Celebrate **ELVIS**

Private Conversations • Never Before Published Interviews • Rumor Busters • Elvis Trivia & Facts • Q&A with Joe

A TCB JOE PUBLISHING PAPERBACK

Celebrate**ELVIS**

Published by TCB Joe Publishing

A division of TCB Joe Enterprises, LLC

Book & Cover Design by Lauren McMullen and The Dream Factory

TCB Joe books may be purchased for
business or promotional use or for special sales.
For more information please write to: info@tcbjoepublishing.com

ISBN: 0-9778945-5-X

Welcome to Celebrate Elvis, the book series that pays tribute to and facilitates a deeper understanding and appreciation of the world's most celebrated entertainer, my friend, Elvis Presley.

In this volume, we will clarify why Elvis sometimes walked around with a jar of peanut butter. We'll also share the truth behind Priscilla's auctioned wedding ring. These topics and many more in this exciting edition of Celebrate Elvis.

This volume is dedicated to my loving wife, Martha, for being a very strong survivor who continues to inspire me each and every day.

-- Joe Esposito

Our deepest gratitude goes out to:

Linda Albanese	Bettina Honig	Matt Shepard
Richard Albanese	Frank Koors	Bil Traynor
Brian Bailey	Glenn Korsinski	Brenda L. Tucker
Wendy Bishop	Corrine Loomis	Markus Wechsler
Christoph Brummer	Michael McLeavy	Anne Wikoswki
Rachel Davis	Fritz Meyer	Jacques from Paris
Steve Farris	Jimmy Orr	Marie from Rome
Mark Gagnon	Mike Piazza	Sara from Washington DC
Michael Holms	Peter Scurge	

■ **TRIVIA ANSWER** / From last question in *Celebrate Elvis Volume 1*

$1 an hour

What Really Happened?

Interview Excerpt with Joe Esposito

Reporter: Mr. Esposito, I have just watched some footage on the Internet that showed you and Charlie Hodge in an interview with Geraldo in which you stated that you found Elvis in the bedroom instead of the bathroom as you said in later interviews. What do you have to say about this?

Joe Esposito: Well, at the time, those days were very emotional, okay? And I was interviewed by a lot of different reporters; that was very hard to do, and it wasn't easy. But naturally in the back of our minds (my mind and everyone's mind), all we could think about was Elvis during those interviews, and out of respect to my friend's memory, I just did not feel it was right to ever say that I found Elvis in the bathroom, on the floor in the undignified way that we had actually found him. I just did not want the people to visually be "seeing" Elvis like that. I was simply protecting my friend. That's basically all there is to it. Back then, the world was not as tolerant and understanding of such things as it is today. ♦

Did You Know?

That when Bill Black once walked out of a recording session, Elvis picked up Bill's Fender electric bass and played the part himself. ♦

■ **TRIVIA QUESTION** / View answer on next page

Who was the person that called Elvis's house identifying himself as a scout for Sun records and asking Elvis if he would be interested in an audition?

What Really Happened?

Interview Excerpt with Joe Esposito

Reporter: Is it true that before Elvis and Priscilla had Lisa Marie he had always wanted a boy who was going to be named John Barron Presley? Can you confirm this?

Joe Esposito: An absolute lie, no way. Elvis never said that he wanted a boy. He was thrilled to have a baby; he loved kids and was so happy when Lisa Marie was born. Elvis never said that he wanted a boy. ♦

Ask Joe

I have a letter here from Lucy J in Missouri.

Lucy says:

Joe, in a DVD series I see a very happy, fun moment with you and Elvis on a tandem bicycle, at the sound stages, during a break. Was that during rehearsal for his pre-Vegas concert, and what do you remember? Thank you very much!

Yes, that was during the pre-Vegas concerts. We were practicing at MGM Sound Stages. That's what it was; we used to ride that tandem around quite a bit while we were doing a series of rehearsal sessions. Before we had to go over to the Colonel's office, we jumped on a bike and went over there; then, after we finished, you see us coming back. We enjoyed doing that quite a bit; it was fun. And that was really just what it was, as you know, Elvis being funny about it when he got off the bike! ♦

■ **TRIVIA ANSWER** / Answer to question on previous page
Scotty Moore

What Really Happened?

Interview Excerpt with Joe Esposito

Reporter: What is the story behind Christina Crawford breaking the cigars that you would light for Elvis?

Joe Esposito: Well, I dated Christina a couple of times, and she was in one of our movies. So, she would come over to the house on occasion, sit around with us, and all that. She did not like cigars, and I didn't know this at the time. So, Elvis would pick up and light a cigar; then Christina would say, "Elvis, I don't like cigars, so would you please put that out?"

He would not stop smoking it, so she reached over and took the cigar out of his mouth, and then she broke it in half. Well, Elvis was not too happy about that, and he got into a little disagreement with her. He told me, "Joe, get her out of here!" So, I took her home, and that was that. It was very embarrassing for me, I'll tell you that. But, you know, what do you do? You just don't know what somebody is going to do or how he or she is going to react! ♦

Did You Know?

That Oscar Davis once worked as an Advance Man for Col. Parker on an Eddy Arnold Show. ♦

■ **TRIVIA QUESTION** / View answer on next page
What was the relationship between Elvis and Buzzy Forbess?

---

[3]

Up Close and Personal:
Elvis and Royalty

A candid conversation between Joe Esposito and Daniel Lombardy

Daniel: There was a picture taken of Elvis and a Princess from Thailand. ... What do you remember about that particular meeting?

Joe: In those days, Hollywood really had a huge draw on celebrities and dignitaries from all over the world, and, like most ordinary people, they also wanted to come and meet different celebrities. So, then the studios would be bringing the guest onto the sets. Basically, that's what happened between Elvis and the Princess from Thailand and a Scandinavian Princess on another time.

So, in a nutshell, different people would come up to Elvis and talk with him before having their pictures taken with him and then make a big deal out of it. It was a normal and regular occurrence. Elvis never called anyone up and said, "Hey, I want to meet the Queen of England..." or anything like that.

[Laughing]

Everyone wanted to meet him!

Wasn't there a time when Elvis was actually invited to meet the Queen of England?

Oh, yeah, he was invited to meet her a few times. But, regrettably, it never materialized. I think that meeting would have been a pretty big one, don't you?

■ **TRIVIA ANSWER** / Answer to question on previous page

They were friends that went to high school together, and both lived at Lauderdale Courts.

I think it would have been another one of Elvis's crowning moments: President Nixon, the Beatles, and then Her Majesty, the Queen of England. I think it would have been an amazing event! ♦

Always On My Mind

My name is Steve Farris, and I reside in Kansas City, Missouri. Aside from listening to his music through Sirius Radio, I often find myself watching TV programs for Elvis references.

A lot of times the old programs on *TVLand* (channel 64) show us things that relate to Elvis. In fact, a week or so back, the currently running television show, *Las Vegas*, devoted their whole episode to Elvis. I also enjoy looking locally for tribute artist performances. On his birthday, both a local station and a bar held a tribute artist performance. I have been on two floats in the local Elvis Parade, and our fan club even won First Prize for our entry of a *Blue Hawaii* theme! Both the parade and its tribute artist show had been sponsored by 97.9-KY and, of course, recently Oprah has had several programs devoted entirely to Elvis.

Lisa Marie has been to KC twice in the past two years. The first time, some of my fan club members and I went to see her. But, the second time, the house was *sold-out* before we had a chance to get tickets! Terry Mike Jeffrey has been at our local Ameristar Casino several times. I've gone to at least two of his shows. He was also on Sirius today, featured in a trivia shoot-out, and he won again. I've seen the Jordanaires twice in concert (once with Jamie Aron Kelley). AND MY OWN DESKTOP ICON IS A PERSONALLY-TAKEN PHOTO OF ELVIS'S ACTUAL LIVINGROOM!!!" LOL :-} ♦

■ **TRIVIA QUESTION** / View answer on next page

What was the occasion that caused Elvis to board an airplane for the first time?

Ask Joe

I have a letter here from Marie in Rome, Italy. Marie says:

Joe, what was the real reason for Elvis getting plastic surgery on his eyes in 1975?

Well, it was not a major thing. He had very small areas underneath his eyes, and it bothered him. It was no big deal; it was just like many people choose to get, a very small procedure when they have that done. It was a very small surgery, no big deal at all; and that was it! ♦

What Really Happened?

Interview Excerpt with Joe Esposito

Reporter: It has been written before that Col. Parker once passed out cigars to a bunch of guys around a roulette table to literally smoke out a pesky and annoying woman who had been lingering there, wanting to play roulette…just to get rid of her. Joe, what really happened there?

Joe Esposito: Now, I never heard that story. I don't think that the Colonel would have done that to a woman. …He would do it to a guy, yes, but no, not to a woman. ♦

Did You Know?

That Elvis owned a horse by the name of Pokey Dunit. ♦

■ **TRIVIA ANSWER** / Answer to question on previous page
To audition for the Arthur Godfrey Show.

What Really Happened?

Interview Excerpt with Joe Esposito

Reporter: It was written that, due to a poor turnout for the first of six scheduled shows for the Houston Astrodome, Elvis was quoted as saying, "Well, that's it. I guess I just don't have it anymore." Tell us, Mr. Esposito, what were the actual circumstances surrounding a poor turnout of only 10,000 people for the first show in an arena that easily held 50,000?

Joe Esposito: I don't know who told you that, but that is a Mount Everest of a big lie. We were packed for all of the Astrodome shows. I don't know how anybody in his or her right mind could claim that there was a poor turnout at the Houston Astrodome; that's just insane! You had a better chance of getting mauled by a grizzly bear in downtown New York City than of getting a ticket to an Elvis concert performance. The arena was already filled by thousands of people who were attending the Houston livestock and rodeo show that, by itself, is a very well-attended annual event. ♦

Did You Know?

That Mae Boren Axton played Elvis her demo of "Heartbreak Hotel" in his room at the Andrew Jackson Hotel in Nashville. ♦

■ **TRIVIA QUESTION** / View answer on next page
Where did the first RCA recording session with Elvis take place?

Ask Joe

I have a letter here from Rachel Davis. She says:

How did the Elvis and Priscilla wedding rings show up for an auction sale? Joe, how could Priscilla do this?

Rachel, I am not sure if I can answer your question. Well, I think Elvis's wedding ring is actually still at Graceland, and, as far as how they got the ring that Priscilla wore, she lost it when we were horseback riding at the Circle G Ranch. We couldn't find it. I think somebody may have found her ring and given it back to Elvis. I can't say for sure, but I think that Elvis might have given the ring to David Stanley's wife. I think they sold it. In my opinion, it is definitely something that Priscilla would not have done. ◆

Always On My Mind

Hi, my name is Michael McLeavy, and I reside in Dana Point, California. All total, I have been living in the United States for about forty-two years. The main reason I came to the United States was to meet Elvis Presley. On July 3, 1965, I left my native Scotland and came to Redondo Beach, California, in the hopes of meeting Elvis in person. Once I arrived, I found out that they were shooting *Paradise Hawaiian Style* at their airport, so I got a break early on! Off on my scooter I went, as it happened to be my only form of transportation at that time. So I went down there expecting to see Elvis, but was told that Elvis had left and that they had wrapped at that particular location.

■ **TRIVIA ANSWER** / Answer to question on previous page
1525 McGavock Street, Nashville, Tenn.

The man said Elvis lived in Bel Air on a street called Perugia Way; I guess that's how you pronounce it. I went to its gate, which was opened by a person in the house. Then I walked up to the house, knocked on the door, and a maid opened the door, telling me Elvis was finished filming and that he already had gone back to Memphis. I asked when he would be back, and she said that he would probably be back in two or three months. Luckily for me, she was kind enough to give me a tour of the house. It was a beautiful, rounded house.

Over the next two or three months, I got to know Sonny West, Jerry Schilling and Richard Davis. They knew that I came all the way from Scotland just to meet Elvis, so they told me to keep trying and to keep coming up to the house and that they would keep an eye out for me. One night I went up to the house, since I had just borrowed a friend's car and promised that I would have it back by ten o'clock in the evening. I remember it was a Saturday night; I'll never forget it. There were boys and gals outside the house. All of a sudden, a big black Rolls Royce pulled up with Sonny driving, and he waved to me. Sonny told me, "Just more or less hold on—there's a good chance you're going to meet Elvis tonight."

So, anyway, Sonny got out of the car and sort of invited me inside the gate. He was able to get me away from the crowd when he told me to just stand right there, that Elvis was just going to have some dinner first. I did as I was asked, and then I waited and waited. Time passed, and it was getting close to ten o'clock.

I knew I had to get the car back; so, reluctantly, I had to leave. Sadly, I missed my chance to meet Elvis that evening. The next day, I called the

---

■**TRIVIA QUESTION** / View answer on next page

Why did Elvis have three TVs in the music room?

studio and spoke to Sonny again. He said, "If you would have hung on a little bit longer, Elvis would have come out to meet you, …but that Elvis had understood what actually happened. …It was just too long, and he had probably thought you had other things to do." [Laughing a lot] Yeah, right! Anyway, Sonny said to me, "Don't panic, just call Tom Diskin at MGM and tell him I told you to call." So, then I called Tom Diskin, and he couldn't have been any nicer when he listened to my story. Then he asked me to call him again on the following day. When I called him back, Tom told me to be at the Racetrack entrance in Torrance, where Elvis would be filming scenes for the movie *Spinout*. I took a day off work, went on location and easily got passed by security, since they already had my name, and so on; then, I was "in".

After awhile, I saw a black Rolls Royce drive up, and it stopped over nearby the trailers where all the friends hung out. Sonny came out and said, "Come on over here with me." He took me down to where they would usually sit during the movie scenes' filming, and then Sonny pointed toward a chair that was on the left side of Elvis's chair. I just could not believe it! So, I'm sitting there and saying, "After all these years of listening to his music, and so on, is this really going to happen?"

Sure enough, here comes Elvis surrounded by all these guys, probably to make sure I was not just some deranged lunatic or crazy man! He came down and said, "Hi Mike! Welcome, and I'm sorry to hear what has happened before. As a host, I apologize." I said, "No problem!" So, he was very generous, and he said, "You go on and sit here." And that was *me* for more or less the next eight to eight-and-one-half hours. I sat there from morning till night. After he had shot a few scenes, Elvis came

---

■ **TRIVIA ANSWER** / Answer to question on previous page
He wanted to watch the 3 major networks at the same time.

back and asked me about Scotland. He told me that, at one point, he briefly touched down in Scotland on his way back to America. He also spoke of the Beatles and the Rolling Stones, and so on.

Anyway, at the end of that day, Elvis actually walked me up to the gate and said he wished me all the best! That is more or less what actually happened. The impression he left me with of how great a guy he truly was will stay with me for as long as I live. ♦

Ask Joe

Frank Koors in Denver, Colorado, writes:

Joe, what was up with that jar of peanut butter we can see Elvis holding when he was coming out of a building before heading towards a waiting limo? Was that a regular habit of his?

No, it wasn't; but Elvis really loved peanut butter, as we all know. It has a lot of good protein in it, and, if you are really hungry, you can just take a couple of tablespoons of it because it fills you up real quick. That is the only reason, really. Elvis did not do that all that often. ♦

Did You Know?

That Jimmy Lot was the first non-Blue Moon Boy to play on an Elvis record. ♦

■ **TRIVIA QUESTION** / View answer on next page
Where did Elvis celebrate his 27th Birthday?

What Really Happened?

Interview Excerpt with Joe Esposito

Reporter: *Is it true that Milton Prell was the front man to the Detroit Mob, who secretly controlled Elvis, through the Colonel, by way of his gambling debts?*

Joe Esposito: Boy, now that is another story that I have personally never heard. Milton being a Mob guy, no! No, we knew him since 1960 and, no, I don't think so, as to him being in the Mob. ♦

Did You Know?

That the statue of Jesus you can still see in the Meditation Garden was given to Elvis as a Christmas present in 1965. ♦

Always On My Mind

My name is Billy Traynor, and I live in Hamburg. For as long as I can remember, I've always been an Elvis fan. I remember watching him on *Elvis: That's The Way It is* in our theaters, and I was awestruck by the man and the persona and especially by the reaction of the fans. I was thinking what a gift from God that Elvis really is! ♦

Did You Know?

That the movie *Double Trouble* was once called *You're Killing Me*. ♦

■ **TRIVIA ANSWER** / Answer to question on previous page
At the Sahara Hotel in Las Vegas.

What Really Happened?

Interview Excerpt with Joe Esposito

Reporter: Is it true that Elvis had a very large teddy bear collection?

Joe Esposito: Elvis had a lot of teddy bears that were sent to him from different places, like given to him onstage. He displayed them in the Trophy Room; there were a lot of teddy bears in there, but they were all given to him by his fans. He got hundreds and hundreds after the song "Teddy Bear" came out. ♦

Always On My Mind

I live in Paris, and my name is Jacques. I love Elvis with every fiber of my being. I even tried to sing like him in front of people once, until I got yanked off the stage! But, that is okay, because at least I can say I tried. My favorite movies are *Jailhouse Rock*, *Love Me Tender* and *Fun In Acapulco*. I really like those. ♦

Did You Know?

That on the USS Arizona Memorial in Hawaii, Elvis and Colonel Parker laid a bell-shaped wreath designed by Col. Parker containing 1,177 carnations, one for each serviceman killed aboard the ship. ♦

■ **TRIVIA QUESTION** / View answer on next page

What caused the filming of *Kid Galahad* to be moved from Hidden Lodge in California back to the Hollywood lot?

Up Close and Personal:
Snowball fights at Graceland

A candid conversation between Joe Esposito and Daniel Lombardy

Daniel: What do you remember about the snowball fights that you all had in Graceland?

Joe: You mean the snowball fights *at* Graceland, right [Laughing]?

[Laughing] Yes, the ones that took place outside the house.

[Both laughing]

Well, basically whenever a snowstorm hit, we would all be out there late at night making snowmen, then havin' snowball fights and creating a big fire in front of the house…breaking the tree branches, having a fire and just hanging outside there all night! It was just a fun thing to do. Elvis was a big kid at heart, and he never had a chance to do any of that stuff when he was actually a young kid.

Right, right.

You know what I'm sayin'…so, when he became successful, this is what he did—those things that he couldn't do when he was young.

What about you, Joe, when you were a kid?

Well, I had snowball fights in Chicago [Laughing]; as you know there's a lot of snow in Chicago!

[Laughing}

■ **TRIVIA ANSWER** / Answer to question on previous page
A snowstorm.

We had guys out in the streets of our neighborhood rolling up snowmen. In fact, I remember in Chicago one time…

Don't tell me you were putting rocks in the snowballs!

[Laughing] It's the truth. We were out in the street, rolling this big snowman that we had to push with a car, because we couldn't push that damn thing anymore [Laughing], but that was us just having fun back in Chicago. But, with Elvis and at Graceland, those snowball fights… yeah, we had fun; we had a ball! ♦

Did You Know?

That Elvis put a call in to President Jimmy Carter to try to help out a friend in a federal court case. ♦

Always On My Mind

I am Bettina Honig from Alsace, France, and I am really in love with Elvis. My mother played Elvis for me when I was in high school, and I have been hooked ever since! Morning, noon and night, I listened to the Elvis music. I cannot imagine what my life would be like without him. I love him very much! ♦

Did You Know?

That Elvis gave Ed Hopper a black eye after Ed pulled a knife on him at a gas station in 1956. ♦

■ **TRIVIA QUESTION** / View answer on next page

Which Memphis Mafia member briefly became the road manager for Brenda Lee after a blowup with Elvis?

What Really Happened?

Interview Excerpt with Joe Esposito

Reporter: Is it true that Elvis gave Barbra Streisand some constructive criticism after seeing one of her shows at the International Hotel? Barbra was supposedly so incensed by this that she swore to get back at Elvis.

Joe, it has also been hinted by people who had access to Barbra that she attempted to lure Elvis into the movie A Star is Born to get his hopes up and offered him a role for a part which Kris Kristofferson was already under contract for. …It was also said that Colonel Parker was on to Barbra early on and saved Elvis a lot of embarrassment by advising Elvis to reject her offer and, thereby, avoided Elvis's being turned down for the part very publicly.

Joe Esposito: That is one orca-sized lie. No such thing. Elvis had never criticized her for anything in her show. They got along fine and, as for Kris having the part already—that is absolutely not true. I know that for a fact; he did not have the part until after Elvis had turned it down. So, I just don't know where the people come up with these stories. It just drives me nuts! There is no truth to that made-up fairytale whatsoever! ♦

Did You Know?

That the movie *Spinout* was once called *Never Say Yes.* ♦

■ **TRIVIA ANSWER** / Answer to question on previous page
Lamar Fike

Ask Joe

This question comes from Peter Scurge in Dublin, Ireland.

Peter asks:

Joe, do you ever remember venturing out into the desert with Elvis while you guys were at Las Vegas during the 70's, either to target shoot or sightsee? And what did Elvis think about the heat in Nevada?

Peter, I'll tell you, we never did really think about the heat while in Las Vegas because we were always busy working as well as performing onstage, which, as you know, was always indoors! But, in Palm Springs, Elvis had a home where he really liked to go out dune buggy riding, especially at night. He had a dune buggy, and so did I, and so we used to go out quite a bit, late at night, when nobody else was around. We had really good times! In fact, I had a bad accident one time. But, as far as the Nevada heat bothering Elvis? No, it did not bother him because, remember, we stayed up all night and didn't go out much during the day, so the heat didn't bother us too much. ◆ (Full dune buggy story in Volume 1 of Celebrate Elvis)

Did You Know?

That Elvis, on an impulse, once took the Greyhound bus to Las Vegas for a trial spin on a weekend while it was being customized by George Barris. ◆

■ **TRIVIA QUESTION** / View answer on next page

In the movie *Kissin' Cousins*, Elvis played the role of both twin brothers. Who was the stand-in for one twins in scenes that required both to appear?

Ask Joe

We have a letter here from Christoph Brummer, a German gentleman.

Dear Mr. Esposito: I'm a big fan of Elvis, and of you, and would like to know if Elvis himself had realized his health problems? And, if so, did he ever talk to you about it? Did you notice he had problems and try to talk with him about that? I've read he didn't even think he had a problem with his drugs. Is that true? Thank you very much, and may God bless you. - Christoph Brummer, Germany

Christoph, we all talked to Elvis about his problems; he did not like to talk to us about them, but we did sit down and discuss these issues many times, individually or in groups. Elvis knew he had some problems, but he always said that he was going to solve them; but he never did. That was Elvis, you know. You could not make him do something that he did not want to do. That is all I can say about that one. ♦

Did You Know?

That Elvis once mentioned these words in an interview with Armed Forces Radio: "I choose songs with the public in mind. I try to visualize it as though I'm buying the record myself." ♦

■ **TRIVIA ANSWER** / Answer to question on previous page
Lance LeGault

Fan Spotlight Interview

With Corrine Loomis

My name is Corrine Loomis, and I'm from Yorba Linda, California.

Daniel Lombardy: Corrine, can you tell us a little bit about what got you into Elvis?

Well, my dad worked for RCA in the fifties and early sixties. So, as a child of about four or five, I would be exposed to all of the records that were popular at that time. I had the 45's of "Heartbreak Hotel" and "Old Shep", so I played those all the time. Then, I kind of moved away from Elvis until his *'68 TV Special*. That was when my interest was piqued again, and I became a die-hard fan from that point on!

I've been traveling over mountains
Even through the valleys, too
I've been traveling night and day
I've been running all the way
Baby, trying to get to you.

■ **TRIVIA QUESTION** / View answer on next page
What year was Elvis awarded his second degree black belt?

Corrine, how old were you when you first saw the special air on TV, and what in particular do you remember from when you first saw it?

Well, let's see, I would have been fourteen. I was born in 1954. I think I was just taken by his energy, by the music and by his great connection with his audience…certainly by how great he looked, and I just really connected with everything about him! That is when everything really kicked in for me.

Corrine, very well said. Ah, what would you consider as being some of your personal top five Elvis songs and Elvis movies?

Well, I think my number one movie would certainly be *That's The Way It Is* because I think it is such a great portrayal of him in concert with the behind-the-scenes footage of him during rehearsals. That was just such a treat, especially back then, when having that raw footage of him was pretty rare! I was mesmerized seeing him in his element, rehearsing; it was very captivating. Regarding his movies, I like the early ones such as *Jailhouse Rock*, *Love Me Tender* and *Kid Galahad*; and I like *Change of Habit* because Elvis just looked so great in that movie. I would consider these my moody favorites. …I mean my movie favorites [Laughing]!

My moody favorites, huh [Laughs]?

Yeah, my movie favorites; and my song favorites…I don't know. …I am sure that you hear this from everyone, Daniel. For me, it would just be impossible to narrow it down to just one, but I really love Elvis's sacred music and his gospel music, especially his recording of "Somebody Bigger Than You and I". That is one of my most favorites ever, along

---

■ **TRIVIA ANSWER** / Answer to question on previous page
1963

with "How Great Thou Art". I think that Elvis just really nailed it on songs like "The Wonder of You" and also "I Really Don't Want to Know"—those kind of bluesy things where his voice was just really so ready to explode, you know? Also, another one I really like is "Kentucky Rain"; also all of Elvis's songs from the Memphis Sessions; that era right there had really captivated me. So, I think that those would really be my favorites.

Those are some really good choices, Corrine. What would you tell Joe if you were speaking with him right now?

I would tell Joe, "Thank you for your loyalty! And, thank you for your love of Elvis and for protecting him, ah, for protecting his memory and most definitely, keeping his memory alive, not only for the fans who were able and fortunate enough to see him, but for the legions of people who have come along as Elvis fans even after he passed away." —for them to be able to have such a stellar person like Joe, whose goal is to protect everything about the memory of Elvis, as well as Joe's ability and dedication to promote the legacy of Elvis and to not do it in a self-serving way. I really believe that Joe Esposito is doing a wonderful thing, not only from the fans' viewpoint. I do think that Elvis would also be very grateful to Joe! But, it's really quite wonderful for all of the fans.

Corrine, what message would you like to share with the newer generation Elvis fans out there, to help perpetuate the memory of Elvis Presley?

I would tell them to really listen to his music and absorb everything that they can about him in the songs he sings; also, to try and get an understanding of Elvis as a total human being because he wasn't *just*

■TRIVIA QUESTION / View answer on next page

What did Danny Thomas buy from Elvis on behalf of St. Judes Hospital?

or *only* a great voice. He was not just "beautiful", that is, a physically beautiful person, and Elvis did not just simply have a wonderful personality; I mean, it was all of those things combined, and in my opinion anyway, there has never been another entertainer who has, or ever will have, embody all those things at the same time! I remember the time when I first saw him in Vegas, Daniel. I had the thrill of actually seeing Elvis in concert nine times there and, most of the time, I sat right up front with my arm on the stage!

Really, nine times? Corrine, I'm impressed.

Yes, I got a scarf and a kiss one time. Elvis was really larger than life; he was so charismatic. I believe that Elvis was really a gift from God for all mankind to enjoy.

You are absolutely correct.

I was never in his presence socially to meet him. But, I can only imagine, from the stories many people have told about his magnetism and powerful presence. For instance, they'd be talking in, say, a living room or in a studio setting when Elvis would very quietly walk in a back door or come down the stairs. People would instinctively and intuitively turn to him after feeling his "presence" suddenly enter into the room.

Sure, Corrine, I know exactly what you mean.

Daniel, I feel that Elvis really touched me deeply for my whole life. His music and his persona are as relevant and important to me today as he was while he was still with us physically. Elvis has been with me through deaths in my family and through a divorce, as well as through heartbreaks. He has been there in both the good times and the bad.

■ **TRIVIA ANSWER** / Answer to question on previous page
The USS Potomac

Elvis is a constant in my life, whose music I can go to for joy and for inspiration. That's just the way it is going to be for me until my dying day!

Considering that you're a detective, I would say that his music is kind of important at times, especially, with some of the characters and traumatic situations you deal with on a regular basis.

Yeah, it really is. I think my job sometimes has what I would say is a cumulative effect, or there are cases where, you know, they will get into your head and really bother you. However, in the end, they don't have that much of an impact on me. Then, all of a sudden, I will work a case that is relatively routine or not as traumatic to the victim, or as emotionally bad, and I will just about have like a meltdown. I think it has a cumulative effect, where it just builds on you; then you just kind of, you know, stuff it down. All of a sudden it seems that one little thing will happen to "trigger" it, and then you've a disproportionate reaction to the case or its situation. Those are some of the moments where the "Elvis magic" in his music has helped me out tremendously. You know, it's almost like it centers me in a weird way! It like pulls me back and centers me by "grounding" me, especially because Elvis was alive when my mother was alive, and she loved him.

My father, of course, only "tolerated" Elvis, but that was half the fun. Do you know what I mean by that [Chuckles]? So, when I think of Elvis, I think of my childhood, and I think of my life and how idyllic it was when I was at that age. I think of my parents, mostly of my mother, who would ride the bus with me to Las Vegas to see him in concert! We would, of course, spend the night and come back the next day.

■ **TRIVIA QUESTION** / View answer on next page

  During which movie did Elvis receive stiches after performing his own stunt?

So, he is, you know, part of the family for all of his fans. Elvis was definitely a part of my family; he was my whole childhood experience, for that matter. I think that is why he is so grafted into me, because I think of all those times with my family. When I think about when Elvis passed, it is very rough because both of my parents passed in that same time in history. So, you know they are all kind of like locked in that little time warp.

I cannot even begin to imagine how that must feel, Corrine!

Daniel, it all happened in that same time frame right there. ♦

Ask Joe

We have Sara in Washington, DC, with the following question:

We know Elvis was a huge movie buff and that he went to a lot of theatres in Memphis. Where did he watch movies when he was either performing in Las Vegas or when on the road while on tour?

Well, when we were on the road, we were always busy doing concerts and shows or events. So, we did not have time to see movies in local theatres very often. The only time we would go out to see movies was at the Malco Theatre in Memphis, where we would rent out the whole place in the evenings. But as far as being on the road in L.A. and places like that, we did not go to the movies. ♦

■ **TRIVIA ANSWER** / Answer to question on previous page

Roustabout

Up Close and Personal: Pat Boone and Elvis

A candid conversation between Joe Esposito and Daniel Lombardy

Daniel: What do you remember about Pat Boone?

Joe: We would meet Pat in the sixties quite a number of different times because Pat was making movies in those days. I remember one time, Pat was there making a movie at 20th Century Fox at the same time we were there shooting. But, I don't remember the name of Pat's movie at the time [Laughing]. On several occasions, we would meet Pat outside a sound stage and play football—not "real" football itself, more like "tag" football—but Pat would often play football with us on fields on the weekends. Pat Boone was a real nice man, a regular guy, just very down-to-earth. Elvis liked him a lot, and Pat really loved Elvis, too!

Did Pat ever come to see any of Elvis's shows in the 70's?

Do you mean in Las Vegas? I don't remember Pat coming to see the show; I just don't remember. That's a good question! ♦

Did You Know?

That Alan Fortas was the foreman in charge of maintenance and livestock for the Circle G Ranch. ♦

■ **TRIVIA QUESTION** / View answer on next page
What was the original title for the movie *Tickle Me*?

Ask Joe

Brenda Laura Tucker from Huntsville, Alabama, asks:

Joe, I have seen a lot of karate photos of Elvis working out and practicing with Red, Dave and several karate champions. Did he ever get injured during practice? I have been practicing karate since I was 13 and have been injured many times over the years, so I always wondered if this was also the case with Elvis. Thank you ...B L

Well, Elvis did get hurt, but not too much when he was working out with the guys. He did get hurt when breaking those damn boards with his hands. And, a couple of times, Elvis hurt his hand pretty bad and was a little bit embarrassed about it. Other than that, there were no serious injuries to speak of. ♦

What Really Happened?

Interview Excerpt with Joe Esposito

Reporter: It was once written that Elvis always wanted to own his own pharmacy. Joe, what do you know about this?

Joe Esposito: [Laughing] Ah, one time he mentioned that. ...But, no—if he really wanted to, he would have done it! ♦

■ **TRIVIA ANSWER** / Answer to question on previous page
Isle of Paradise

Up Close and Personal:
Elvis and Sam Thompson

A candid conversation between Joe Esposito and Daniel Lombardy

Joe: Well, Elvis loved Sam Thompson. Sam was and is a good guy! He is very smart and very, very loyal. Sam is just a good guy, and Elvis really liked him a lot. You know that Elvis got to know Sam because of his sister, Linda Thompson, okay?

Daniel: Okay.

Sam used to hang around us a little bit when he was working with the Memphis Police Department. And, as you know, Elvis had always loved police officers. I mean, he really loved law enforcement, you know that, Daniel....

I sure do!

So, that's one of the reasons that Elvis asked Sam to go to work for him in security. Naturally, Sam didn't turn Elvis down; and that is how it all started. From that time on, Sam was with us all the way up until Elvis passed away. In fact, even after Linda had left Elvis in 1976, Sam was still there working with us!

What were some of the things that Sam did around Elvis, in terms of the tours and things like that, and what would his job have involved?

Sam was a security guy; he worked security with us. Sam, Red West, Sonny West and Ed Parker, people like that, all worked together when it

---

■**TRIVIA QUESTION** / View answer on next page
Which session players where added to the soundtrack recording of "Harum Scarum" to give the music more of a middle eastern feel?

came to Elvis's arrival or departure from buildings and all of those hotels, making sure exactly which way we would go out and, of course, that we all walked out together! They also set up security at all the arenas; help was always available if we needed it. That is exactly what their job was, and it was a very specific job, Daniel. ♦

What Really Happened?

Interview Excerpt with Joe Esposito

Reporter: Is it true that, at one time, Elvis had asked Chips and the American group that worked for him, to be Elvis's official band in Vegas?

Joe Esposito: No, that is not true at all. Elvis had his TCB band, and that was it. No, that was never mentioned.

Was Chips ever considered before you set the wheels in motion to have James Burton form the TCB band?

No, no, not at all. ♦

Did You Know?

That the last movie Elvis did with Hal Wallis was *Easy Come, Easy Go*. ♦

■ **TRIVIA ANSWER** / Answer to question on previous page
Rufus Long and Ralph Strobel on flute and oboe.

Fan Spotlight Interview

With Matt Shepard

Daniel Lombardy: What got you into Elvis, and how did Elvis influence your life?

Matt: Well, OK, I was very young although, I mean, I was in school when Elvis died back in '77. And, back then we had only about three TV channels available in the UK. I was just pressing the buttons on the TV, trying to find something of interest. All of sudden there was this guy singing with a guitar by a swimming pool, surrounded by bikini-clad girls. So, even at the tender age of about five or six I thought, "Ooooh yeah, I can do that too [Laughing]!"

[Laughs]

Obviously, I turned to my family and asked, "Who's this guy on the TV?" And my uncle answered, "Oh, that is Elvis Presley!" I had never heard of him before, but I immediately sensed while I was watching him that this guy's very cool. At that time, I didn't know anything about him, other than that he was in a film, and my uncle said, "Well, I've got a mate who makes posters. I know he's got some Elvis posters on his end of a list, so I will send you one!" And, sure to his word, a couple weeks later, I received this life-size picture of Elvis…a shot of him wearing his teddy bear outfit, you know, the one from *Loving You*.

Right.

That picture adorned my bedroom door for years. I can also remember that, at the time, RCA had a budget record label called Camden, which

---

■ **TRIVIA QUESTION** / View answer on next page
Which Memphis Mafia member bought himself a Triumph 650 motorcycle that inspired Elvis to buy a fleet of cycles?

was just bringing out albums with some of the "Elvis is Back" Capital Records' songs. There was an item called "Return to Sender", and I remember we got it from our local Woolworth's store—I think it's called Wal-Mart in America. I think it cost one pound ninety-nine brand new, plus it came with a free poster! So, the first Elvis song that I ever heard on a record player was that one. And I was mistaken when I thought that Elvis was saying, "Return To Cynder".

[Laughing]

Oh, Cynder…must be a place in America!

[Laughs louder]

And that's my earliest memory of an Elvis song.

[Laughs]

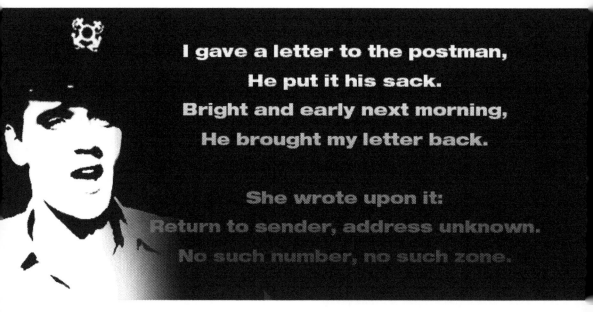

I gave a letter to the postman,
He put it his sack.
Bright and early next morning,
He brought my letter back.

She wrote upon it:
Return to sender, address unknown.
No such number, no such zone.

■ **TRIVIA ANSWER** / Answer to question on previous page
Jerry Schilling

[Laughs] I am completely telling you the truth. None of this is made up, I promise you that, Daniel [Laughs]!

No, no, I haven't heard that one as yet [Laughs]!

Oh, you're always going to think that this next comment is silly; but it was very bizarre, because my mom and dad were a little concerned by the fact that I was really getting into Elvis's music, because we're talking the early 1980's. As you know, by then, Elvis had been passed away almost five years already, and it was really strange because my parents were like, "God, he's going to get to school, and his classmates are going to take the mickey straight out of him!"

Did you say they were going to take "the mickey" out of you?

Well yeah, I mean, when you're like five or six years old at school back in the early eighties, bands popular back in the UK were groups like Madness and The Jamm, and there's a guy called Shakin' Stevens who actually plays Elvis in the West Bank in London. So, they were trying to get me into Shakin' Stevens' band, because they thought he was possibly the nearest to Elvis [Laughs] that the UK has got. But it didn't work... bless their minds. So, my parents gave up and haven't bothered trying since [Laughs].

[Laughs]

I love them dearly, but now they just put up with me being an Elvis fan.

Matt what would you consider your top five Elvis movies?

My top five Elvis movies? Okay, well the first, as my earliest memory, it

---

■ **TRIVIA QUESTION** / View answer on next page
At one point in Elvis's career he received a telegram from 90 RCA executives. What was on this telegram?

turns out was the one I watched on the TV—*Girls! Girl! Girls!* So, I do definitely have to put that one in my top five, and I think that *Loving You* would rank right up there with my most favorite ones. During that movie, it's the closest that we got to see the real rock 'n' roll side of Elvis. I am really fond of his film *Tickle Me*, probably because it had a load of songs that Elvis had already recorded for album tracks; and he didn't actually record anything new for the film, since they dug out some really good studio tracks from 1961 that they used for that movie almost four years later. I think songs like "It's a Long, Lonely Highway" are really his top-caliber stuff. I thought the film was very funny too because Elvis was really, really good at his comic timing; so that is also a favorite one. I liked *Follow That Dream* a lot probably because of its similar comic values. I think, as well, another movie I really enjoy is *Stay Away Joe*, one of the films a lot of people crucified because it was toward the end of his film career! Yes, that was a very, very funny film, and it boasted a really good supporting cast as well. Again, the few songs that Elvis sang were very good. So, I know these are unusual choices, but I'd say that they are my favorite ones.

Matt, those are some great selections! Let me now ask you the same question in terms of music…your top ten favorite songs?

Oh my God! Can I have five hundred [Laughing]?

[Laughs]

How many choices do I have?

Ten. Ten. Ten [Laughs].

■ TRIVIA ANSWER / Answer to question on previous page

"Your understanding and cooperation made 1965 the biggest of all ten years you have been with us."

Oh, okay, um, right. Then I would say "If I Can Dream" and "Suspicious Minds" are definitely two.

Why do you like "If I Can Dream"?

It's when you read about why and how the song was written. It was actually written overnight, but it captured the mood of America, you know, with Martin Luther King, Jr., and Robert Kennedy both having been assassinated in that same year. It was also the first time Elvis really took a stand to record what he wanted to record in spite of what was suggested that he focus on singing, which was a Christmas song. They came up with "If I Can Dream", and I think that it was really the closest Elvis ever came to recording what seems like a "protest" song. It was absolutely brilliant. Vocally, he was so strong in that song.

I was watching its footage and thinking about the idea of Elvis dressed in white, without the red necktie. It's just incredible; and when it comes back, and you gawk at the "ELVIS" name in big red letters behind it, it becomes quite an iconic video, I would say. So that has just got to definitely be one of them. "Suspicious Minds" is absolutely one of the ultimate Elvis songs. Again, after the movie years, he went back onstage in 1969, when he started to wear all those amazing jumpsuits. He was a lean-mean love machine! He captured and conquered Vegas. Think about that significance. Everyone at the time said Vegas belonged to Sinatra and The Rat Pack. Elvis just came in and shattered all box office records even in January, which is the slowest time of year in Las Vegas. So, to me, the music he performed there was the absolute pinnacle of his return to the stage. It resulted in sold-out concerts from then on.

How true, Matt.

■ **TRIVIA QUESTION** / View answer on next page
In which movie does Elvis play a Navy Seal?

**We can't go on together
With suspicious minds
And we can't build our dreams
On suspicious minds**

As for number three, I have to say that one of my personal favorites was the really early stuff that he did, such as "Blue Moon of Kentucky". I absolutely love Elvis's version of that song, because he took a bluegrass song and literally turned it up a notch. He really sped it up, and it worked so well. Elvis recorded "That's All Right Mama" with Bill Black, Scotty Moore and Stanford, all of whom, as you know, were buzzing after recording that. So, then they did "Blue Moon of Kentucky" for Sam Phillips, and it was just an amazing sound that was never again captured at RCA. It was almost a sacred sound that Elvis took away with him to the grave, unfortunately.

I would say another song I really love is "Way Down", and again Elvis just went back to his roots. You know, he forgot the old Castro arrangements, and he just literally went back to basics with drums and

■ **TRIVIA ANSWER** / Answer to question on previous page
Easy Come, Easy Go

the guitars. "Way Down" was and is just an incredible song. It's rightly so a number one hit even though it was a posthumous spot for Elvis in the UK. It just illustrates Elvis's having literally gone full circle back to basics. To me, that's along similar lines as "Promised Land". I mean to take a song that somebody like Chuck Berry wrote and add something to a song that is already a classic, and then to take it to greatness is something that only Elvis could do. He could always take a song, no matter who else had recorded it, and make it his own. I think with "Promised Land" in 1974, it showed that Elvis could still rock with the best of them. That was just an amazing song, and it definitely goes down as one of my favorites. Another song...aw, gosh Daniel, you're putting me on a spot here [Laughs]…

Of course [Laughs]

Another song I like—I like a lot of the B-sides of the UK singles—is "Devil in Disguise". And, again, when Elvis was recording ballads in the mid-sixties, he then comes out with "Please Don't Drag This String Around", a really great B-side. I loved it; it was just an absolutely great rock 'n' roll song. Speaking of the fans of rock 'n' roll songs, one of my favorite albums has just got to be "Elvis is Back". It's highly under-rated, bizarrely enough, but it was just a good album that has become a bit of a tall classic amongst the fans, I do believe, over the years. There were so many good songs. One of my favorites would have to be "Such A Night", which again, is a song that Elvis took and made "his own"! Right at the end of it was like this big "Wooooh", because they were all obviously completely drained from giving it they're all, but at the same time, really elated from making such a great rock 'n' roll record.

■ **TRIVIA QUESTION** / View answer on next page

When Elvis was a private in the Army, one of his principle duties was that of a jeep driver. What was the name of the person he drove around?

Obviously, all the love songs as well were really fantastic. I think that "Don't Cry Daddy" is a lovely song; again, sort of from the Memphis Sessions of 1969. You could pick any song from the Memphis Sessions of 1969, and they were all just classics in their own right. "Don't Cry Daddy" is an absolutely brilliant song, obviously. I think it was for the 25th Anniversary when Lisa Marie appeared on stage at the big tribute concert for Elvis in Memphis.

Right.

Singing that song with her dad on the screen, I think, makes it even more special for the fans, even though it's never been officially released. That was a very special moment for Elvis and his daughter, Lisa Marie, to be appearing together there for the first time. Daniel, would you let me please say one more…this is hard, I tell you [Laughing].

[Laughs]

[Laughs] One more song—let me think, tell you what—I'm going back to the "Promised Land" album because that's one of my favorite albums, and Elvis did a song that was on that album called "Goodtime Charlie's Got the Blues", which was a really beautiful love song; but it is also a very sad song. There are some very lovely words in it, I think, you know, just again proving in 1974 that Elvis was still *king* of the recording world, because he kept coming out with these amazing songs. So, I think those would have to be the ones right off the top of my head, Daniel. With Elvis's music, I could obviously list a lot more [Laughs].

I have two other songs I would like your take on. The first one is "And I Love You So", and then the second is "My Babe", which was done on opening night '69 in Vegas.

■ **TRIVIA ANSWER** / Answer to question on previous page

Staff Sergeant Ira Jones.

Oh my, yeah, "My Babe" is a really great rocker tune, isn't it? And it's a really good song really. I suppose that Elvis should have recorded it much earlier, you know. I sensed that he jumped on the rock 'n' roll bandwagon a bit more with that song because it really is a timeless number. I mean, again, the opening in Las Vegas in '69, when he did the "Little Sister" and "Get Back" medley, was just great. You know, Elvis up onstage with a guitar and all—it was absolutely brilliant. Because, I mean, he tipped his hat to the Beatles in tribute. But, again, when he recorded something, it was already established as a great hit since Shirley Bassey had done it, then the Beatles had done it, and now Elvis would make his own version of this fantastic song!

"Hey Jude" was another piece right behind it.

Yes! I mean Elvis did it "live" didn't he?

He sure did, Matt.

His version was fantastic! When you hear him singing it onstage, he only kind of does like the first verse and goes into the chorus, which he repeats right away; and the only time you hear him singing that song in its complete version is in the studio.

You are exactly right!

Daniel, can you imagine how incredible it would have been if Elvis had performed the full song onstage?

It would have been really amazing, that's for sure.

He really did a heck of a lot with that song.

■ **TRIVIA QUESTION** / View answer on next page
Where was the press conference for the Houston Astrodome show held?

He sure did. Matt, what's your take on "And I Love You So"?

That was the Perry Como hit, wasn't it? Yeah, I really liked Elvis's rendition of a timeless song, which they had recorded right around the time that Elvis and Priscilla were breaking up. So that song was almost haunting, wasn't it?

Very powerful to say the least; he really does lay into the piece and grab you by your soul.

Again, I think it's a highly underrated song, just like quite a lot of the material that he covered in the early 70's! Possibly because of the tremendous popularity of songs such as "The Wonder of You" and "American Trilogy" or "Burning Love", songs like "And I Love You So", along with "The First Time Ever I Saw Your Face", seem to have been pushed a bit out of the way. That is a shame because they're some of the strongest love songs he did in the 70's.

You are dead on, Matt. Let me ask you, if you had a message to convey to the Elvis fans out there, what would it be?

I would say that Elvis fans are the luckiest fans in the world because we have just got so many great choices when it comes to his music. He might have been gone nearly 30 years, but my goodness me, look at the musical legacy he left us—all those fantastic lyrics and melodies!

Elvis also covers a variety of different genres. Who other than Elvis did that? Sure they call him the King of Rock 'n' Roll, but he went into so many different areas. His gospel music is absolutely magical, and so are his many love songs, and also his country music. It's a shame he never actually recorded a blues album, because his blues music was absolutely

---

■ **TRIVIA ANSWER** / Answer to question on previous page

The Astroworld Hotel

incredible. He could perform the blues along with the best of them. So, being an Elvis fan myself, I think we are all very fortunate to have so much choice. Sometimes, I am amazed at some of the things that come out; just as you think that you have heard it all, more material comes out! And, you can now listen to studio outtakes, you know. Elvis was goofing around and laughing in the studio.

It just takes you back in time to the moments when it was actually happening. I think that, in his life, Elvis was so inaccessible in the UK because, unfortunately, he never toured here. Again, now, thanks to several record labels, as well as thanks to Graceland being open, and *special* thanks to people, like Joe Esposito, who shared these valuable insights, their memories, their websites and their books. It gives the fans access to the person behind the image. It is all so very exciting, and I really do look forward to what is yet to come! ♦

Did You Know?

That Elvis and Priscilla obtained their $15.00 marriage license at the Clark County Courthouse in Las Vegas. ♦

■ **TRIVIA QUESTION** / View answer on next page
What was Elvis's favorite ice cream flavor?

Did You Know?

That Elvis missed Jerry Schilling's wedding because he was recuperating from a fall. ♦

Ask Joe

Markus Wechsler from South Tyrol, (near Austria), writes:

When Elvis had been checked into the hospital in Memphis for exhaustion, they would always hang silver tinfoil over all of the windows. Why did the hospital do that?

Well, the reason for that was because, you know, we were "night people". We stayed up during the nighttime hours and slept during the day. With foil covering, the sunlight would not come into the room, and Elvis could sleep better during the daytime. We did that not just in hospitals, but also in hotels and really everywhere we stayed. It let Elvis and us all sleep better; so that is why we did that! ♦

Did You Know?

That Elvis once told journalist May Mann that he would always keep Graceland because of his mother. ♦

■ **TRIVIA ANSWER** / Answer to question on previous page
Vanilla

Did You Know?

That the Police Chief for San Diego, California, threatened to jail Elvis for disorderly conduct in 1956. ♦

Ask Joe

We have a question from Brian Bailey.

During the concert years you could notice band-aids on Elvis's fingers. Were his fingers or hands damaged?

No, the bandages were placed around the fingers on which Elvis had a ring, because sometimes he would be shaking hands out in the audience, and the ring would almost fall off his fingers. The band-aids kept them from falling, and if someone wanted to try to steal a ring from Elvis's fingers, they could not do that either. That's why you see band-aids around only his ring fingers. So, that is all there was to that. ♦

Did You Know?

That Orchestra Leader Joe Guercio was the key person who had immortalized the "2001 Space Odyssey" adaptation into an opening sequence of every Elvis show. ♦

■ **TRIVIA QUESTION** / View answer on next page
Why did Elvis dye his hair black?

Up Close and Personal:
Elvis and Roy Hamilton

A candid conversation between Joe Esposito and Daniel Lombardy

Daniel: What do you remember about Elvis and Roy Hamilton at the studio? I know that you have a very rare picture of Roy Hamilton that you published in several of your books. What do you remember of the time when Elvis met with him?

Joe: All I knew was before Elvis met Roy, he had always tremendously admired the way Roy sang. Elvis loved Roy's voice and the songs he sang. Then, one day Elvis found out Roy would also be recording at the same studio; so Elvis arranged to meet Roy! When they were introduced, they shook hands and talked a little while. I knew Elvis was thrilled to meet him; he really was! Just like when a fan got to meet Elvis, he just wanted to meet Roy. I mean, he idolized Roy Hamilton, and so he was just very thrilled. They did not talk for long, since both of them were there recording. They just hung out for a little bit, and that was it!

Did they ever meet again, after that first time?

I don't think we ever ran into him again, not while I was around. I don't think so. ♦

Did You Know?

That Comedian Nipsey Russell replaced Sammy Shore. ♦

■ TRIVIA ANSWER / Answer to question on previous page

He dyed his hair black because he admired how good Tony Curtis's hair looked. He felt it would make his eyes stand out more.

Ask Joe

I have a letter here from Jimmy Orr in Easley, SC.

Joe, I've always been very curious about the following question for many, many, years. When the opening scenes of "This Is Elvis" were filmed, what had gone through your mind, as you had to re-create those on location scenes using Elvis's Stutz and then the Elvis bedroom and bathroom scenes? That must surely have been a "much too close for comfort" time for you!

Well, Jimmy, you know, it was definitely not easy, because it was only a few years after Elvis had passed away that we made the movie. And, yes, it was very tough, especially going up into that bathroom and having to re-create those scenes. But, I knew that I had to do it even though it was very difficult. It brought back some very bad memories for me. That is all I can tell you. ♦

Did You Know?

That the documentary *Elvis On Tour* would go on to be named a co-winner of a Golden Globe as Best Documentary of 1972. ♦

■ **TRIVIA QUESTION** / View answer on next page
Who came up with the idea of adding capes to the jumpsuits?

Up Close and Personal:
Elvis and Jimmy Carter

A candid conversation between Joe Esposito and Daniel Lombardy

Daniel: Elvis once met Jimmy Carter and his wife Rosalynn before going onstage. What do you remember about that?

Joe: Well, the Colonel set it up for Jimmy Carter and his wife to come backstage. You know that Elvis always really liked to meet famous people, especially people that truly changed people's lives and stuff like that. So, Elvis was really thrilled to meet him! It was not a long meeting since we were about to do a show. Jimmy Carter came backstage with his wife and several other relatives, along with his own security, friends and family. They took some pictures, and, well, that was basically the extent of their meeting!

He wasn't the President at the time, was he?

No, no. He was the Governor at that time.

So, did he have a Secret Service detail around him at the time?

No, it was not a secret service group, but he did have security personnel.

So he did have security then.

Oh, yeah, usually the Governors have their Sheriff's Department or something like that take care of their security. That's their typical security.

Right, right, I got it! ♦

■ **TRIVIA ANSWER** / Answer to question on previous page
Bill Belew

Up Close and Personal:
Elvis and His Ankle Length Boots

A candid conversation between Joe Esposito and Daniel Lombardy

Daniel: Elvis used to wear ankle length boots. Joe, were those boots customized, or was that just something that was popular and "in" at the time?

Joe: They were like flamenco boots; do you remember flamenco boots?

Yes, I sure do [Laughing].

Yes, Elvis really liked those boots, and sometimes they had the higher heel.

Yep...

That made him a little taller, and then he could put a lift into the shoe to make him even taller! Besides, Elvis just seemed to like the "looks" of that boot. Then, once he got hooked on that style, that's all we used to buy for him to wear! As far as shoes go.

Where did he get those? Was there a particular place you guys bought them?

Now, that I can't remember. I can't tell you which store we bought those in because there was no special or particular place where we would buy those boots. Elvis saw them while we were out shopping one day. I don't remember where the hell we were, whether it was in California or Memphis or where [Laughing], and he saw a pair, liked 'em and bought 'em. And once he tried them out for a while, he felt they were really comfortable, and that was it! ♦

■ **TRIVIA QUESTION** / View answer on next page

Who came up with the idea of surrounding Elvis with his friends on the tiny stage on the *'68 Comeback Special?*

Up Close and Personal:
Bobby Darin and Elvis

A candid conversation between Joe Esposito and Daniel Lombardy

Daniel: Joe, what can you tell me about Bobby Darin? What do you recall about them meeting?

Joe: All that I know is, when I first met Elvis in Germany, I do remember him playing a lot of Bobby Darin songs all the time. He thought Bobby Darin was so talented. I agree with Elvis on that—he really was! Bobby was a talented musician, singer and master entertainer onstage; he was considered basically the white Sammy Davis, Jr., and Elvis loved him; in fact, he idolized him. Elvis thought that he was fabulous, and we used to go see his shows, particularly while he performed in Hollywood, playing at Ciro's on Sunset Blvd, or different Los Angeles clubs, or even in Vegas when Bobby was playing there before Elvis started to play there. That is when we all were just hanging out to have a good time, and we would often go backstage and talk to Bobby; but we didn't hang out with him that much, as far as socializing goes. We just loved to go see his shows, then go backstage to say hello and talk for just a little while; then that was it. Sadly, as you know, Bobby died at a very young age. ♦

Did You Know?

That Elvis was the first person to contribute to the Kui Lee Cancer Fund. ♦

Ask Joe

I have a letter here from Michael Holms who lives in Paris, France.

Hey Joe! It was great seeing you in Memphis.

My question is this: What was the atmosphere around the family and the Memphis Mafia every time Elvis would get checked into the hospital for exhaustion in the 70's? How did everyone handle that and how on earth did the Memphis Mafia provide security while Elvis was a patient?

Well, first of all, we all knew that Elvis would get right back into shape after he had been to the hospital for certain things. We didn't really worry about it, 'cause we were sure it was nothing too serious. So, it was no big deal! Elvis went into the hospital many times, you know, for exhaustion, for checkups and different things.

As far as security, we would always have an extra room right next door set aside for us. So, we would have security, of course, posted right outside the doors at all hours and at all times. We always knew who every person in the area was, you know—nurses and staff like that. So, it would have been very, very difficult for people to just walk right in. During those times, security was not a problem for us at all. ♦

Did You Know?

That Elvis played an explosive ordnance disposal specialist in *Easy Come, Easy Go.* ♦

■ **TRIVIA QUESTION** / View answer on next page
Who was Vince Everett, and what role did he play in Elvis's life?

What Really Happened?

Interview Excerpt with Joe Esposito

Reporter: What would you say is the public's biggest misconception about Colonel Parker?

Joe Esposito: Well, I think the worst misconception about Colonel Parker and Elvis's relationship is that he supposedly controlled Elvis's every move regardless of how small. That's just not true. Elvis had his own mind and had his own group around him; he did what he wanted to do. Colonel had never interfered with Elvis's personal life. A lot of the people say that he did. That's not true. Those people were not there; I was there, and so were a lot of other people. Yes, I'm not saying that Colonel Parker was perfect. He was a human; he made his mistakes like the rest of us. But their relationship was very good over all of those years they spent together. They were a team as far as I'm concerned. Colonel Parker, as we all know, dedicated his life to Elvis Presley from day one—from the time he became his manager. Unlike other celebrity managers who handled a lot of other artists simultaneously, Colonel only took care of Elvis. He had opportunities to get other big-name stars that asked him to manage them, 'cause they saw what he did for Elvis. He turned them all down, and he said, "I give 100% of my time to Elvis." ♦

Did You Know?

That Elvis gave Jack Lord's wife the original belt that belonged to the American Eagle Jumpsuit. ♦

■ **TRIVIA ANSWER** / Answer to question on previous page
Elvis played Vince Everett in *Jailhouse Rock*.

Up Close and Personal:
The Vegas Suite

A candid conversation between Joe Esposito and Daniel Lombardy

Daniel: Let's talk about the Vegas suite Elvis stayed in while he was performing in Las Vegas at the International. Could you please describe the rooms?

Joe: What I remember of the Penthouse Suite is that it was probably the biggest suite in Las Vegas at that time, at about 10,000 square feet. It was on the thirtieth floor, with one side overlooking the Vegas Strip; on the other side, there was a nightclub. Thankfully, the club was far enough away so we could not hear noise or anything.

So, the nightclub was up there when we first opened up, and then you would walk through two big doors into the suite. You first entered into a huge room; at the time, it was yellow and blue. You then walked down three steps into this huge living area. I remember there was a large section that had couches and regular TVs. Its window ran the full length of our suite, so we could overlook the entire city. On the other side, we had a big dining room area that included a professional kitchen, which the personal chefs of the stars who stayed in the suite could use to prepare the restaurant-caliber meals!

The Elvis bedroom was really big and had its own separate and very nice living area that came with a sitting area where guests and friends could relax, talk and have meetings. There were two bathrooms that were also situated in that area. On another wing there were three other bedrooms. The first was the one I stayed in, Charlie Hodge had the second one,

---

■ **TRIVIA QUESTION** / View answer on next page
In how many Elvis movies did DJ Fontana appear?

and Sonny West had the third one. That's where we all lived while Elvis performed in Las Vegas. The rest of the entourage had their separate hotel rooms located throughout the hotel.

So, that was basically the Penthouse, Daniel. The only way you could get up there was by using a certain key. Then, once you got up there, you would always see security on duty, making sure that no "uninvited" guests came knocking on the Penthouse doors.

Well, that would make sense!

So, security was out there all the time, and we always entered the area by the "back" way. We would take a separate service elevator to go down to the stage. The Penthouse Suite was where we lived, and we really had a lot of good times there! ♦

Ask Joe

Hi Joe, my name is Anne Wilkoswki from Michigan.

We always hear how much Sun Studios did for Elvis. Did Elvis ever actually visit Sun Recording Studios after he made it big?

Oh, yes, Elvis really loved Sam Phillips. He and Sam remained good friends for many years, all the way up until Elvis passed away. He had loved that Studio and would visit it periodically. Elvis really appreciated it all because he knew that was where everything had started; so he was very fond of going to the Sun Recording Studios! ♦

■ **TRIVIA ANSWER** / Answer to question on previous page
4 movies

Up Close and Personal: Graceland

A candid conversation between Joe Esposito and Daniel Lombardy

Daniel: What do you remember about Graceland, during the time Elvis was still around?

Joe: Well, basically, most of it is pretty much still the exact same way that it was when Elvis was living there. Several years ago, I had noticed some changes, especially on the rooms out by where their garages used to be. Now they have rooms and offices in that area! But basically, the inside and the upstairs layout are pretty much the same way they were when Elvis lived there.

Okay, how about a "mental" tour of the upstairs. What could a person expect to see if he or she went upstairs?

Well, when you go up the stairs you would turn to the right, and you would see a door, okay?

Okay.

In the beginning the area was open; it wasn't closed in for the longest time. But, then, Elvis decided to make it a private suite that involved one of the bedrooms being turned into a closet. When the suite was created, they had also installed a soundproof wall that kept noise from downstairs coming into the suite. As you know, Elvis slept during the day; so to prevent his being awakened, he had the soundproof wall installed. Now, once you got through the main door, you would see two big double doors on the left. They too were padded in leather to help with the soundproofing.

■**TRIVIA QUESTION** / View answer on next page

Which Florida judge told Elvis to remove his objectionable hip movements from his act?

After you got inside that room, you could see Elvis's bedroom to the right. To the left, you would see the room that Elvis would use as his office. It had a big desk, sound system and all that stuff in there. We used to listen to a lot of demos in that room. That's where Elvis would decide which songs he would record or not. But, his bedroom was a big bedroom, which was also padded in leather, 'cause we were all crazy [Laughing a lot]!

[Laughing]

It was like a nuthouse, you know, so you couldn't hurt yourself and all [Laughing], but it was in red and black, with blackout curtains on all the windows, so that very little light would get in. Elvis had two television sets installed into the ceiling, so you could watch if you were lying down. All you had to do was look straight up, and you would see two TVs.

Very Interesting!

Interesting, yeah, I know [Laughing].

[Laughing]

It was really bizarre [Laughing]! Believe it or not, Daniel, the bed was also padded [Laughing]. Its size was 9 feet by 9 feet, entirely custom-made, including the sheets! It had a black leather headboard, built so that you could pull down these leather arms that would bring out the back of the headboard a little; so, it was almost like sitting in a chair. Elvis could then sit up and watch TV.

Right, right.

■ **TRIVIA ANSWER** / Answer to question on previous page

Judge Marion Gooding

So, when I say there were two TVs in the ceiling, there was also a big TV at the foot of Elvis's custom bed with a stereo.

You could also see his clothes dresser, and to the right of the bed was Elvis's private bathroom. When you go past the built-in shower, you could see a big walk-in closet. Next was the bedroom where I had stayed when I first moved in at Graceland. It was later turned into a big closet space. And besides that, there was Lisa's bedroom. I'm not sure of the layout, but her room also had a nice bathroom. Lisa's room overlooked the backyard, and Elvis's bedroom overlooked the front of the house.

Lisa had a white round bed, right?

She did, yeah, a white one! It had this round top and like this fur thing. It was pretty cute for a kid. There was also a door up there that led to the attic. Now the attic had a lot of stuff up there which Elvis had over the years, like all his military stuff, along with a lot of personal stuff from the past years. His mother's stuff was up there too. I'm sure that a lot of the stuff is still up there now. Actually, it's probably been placed into the museum by now.

Was there anything special about Elvis's private shower or his bathroom?

Well, at that time, it was custom-made with a very large and open shower, which didn't have any glass doors. It was really big, decorated with these little tiles, and it was curved. It was big, but it was a basic shower; there was nothing special about it.

If you remember *This is Elvis…*

■**TRIVIA QUESTION** / View answer on next page

Which key person in Elvis's life at one time worked as an animal officer for the Tampa Humane Society?

... Yes?

You can see a scene leading right up to the bedroom. That was the *only* time that the Presley family allowed anything to ever be filmed upstairs. That is the actual bedroom!

So, that was the real thing!

Right, that is the "real deal". ♦

Ask Joe

Ed asks:

How good was Elvis at karate? Could he have beaten Red or Sonny West in a "straight" fight?

Well, personally, I believe that Elvis could have. But, that would never have happened anyhow, and we will never, ever know, Ed, in my opinion, from what I have witnessed by observing what Elvis could do. ♦

Did You Know?

That Al Strada worked as a security guard at the Monovale house before he began working with Elvis. ♦

■ **TRIVIA ANSWER** / Answer to question on previous page
Col. Tom Parker

Ask Joe

I have a letter from Wendy Bishop.

She writes:

Dear Joe, I was wondering if you were present at the 1995 Elvis concert when the "Don't Cry Daddy" video with Lisa Marie was premiered? What were your feelings...and wouldn't it be wonderful if that "duet" could actually be commercially released? It honestly devastated me even seeing it on YouTube, small screen, etc., and I cannot imagine what it must have been like with everyone there, full screen, etc.

Well, I was there when it was shown five years ago on the Twenty-Fifth Anniversary of Elvis's passing away. That event was truly amazing and unbelievable. There were some legal reasons why they could not release it as a video or a soundtrack. I don't know, maybe they can get that straightened out; but I thought it was absolutely fabulous! They had to play it two or three times because people kept saying, "More, more."...So, it was a pretty amazing event to see. Lisa was very nervous about it, but she did a great job, and it was really fantastic seeing it *live* that year. ♦

Did You Know?

That Elvis was appointed as a Special Deputy Sheriff in Shelby County in 1964. ♦

■ **TRIVIA QUESTION** / View answer on next page
During which grade did Elvis get enrolled at Humes High School?

Fan Spotlight Interview

with Richard and Linda Albanese

Daniel Lombardy: Okay, why don't we start off with you telling the readers a little bit about yourselves; and, of course, starting with Linda, having her tell a little bit about herself…what got her into Elvis; then, when she's done talking, she probably can give you the nod and, Richard, you tell the fans a little bit about yourself…what got you into Elvis. Then, what I'll do is to weave both of you back into the conversation, okay?

Richard: Very good.

Daniel: With those words we'll start off with Linda [Laughing]!

Linda: Great! I was eight years old, and Elvis was appearing on the Ed, no, the Steve Allen show. My sister called me and said, "Hey, come take a look at this young man singing," and that was it for me. I was hooked, cooked [Laughing].

Daniel: You were hooked [Laughing]?

Linda: I was hooked. Daniel. When I saw him dancing and heard his music—most of all, the look of him—I was madly in love at eight years old if you can believe that! Each and every time he appeared on any show, I was sitting right in front of the TV.

Daniel: I can already see you sitting in front of the boob tube all lit up like a Christmas tree [Laughing]!

Linda: [Laughing]…you're right, [Laughing] back then TV was all black and white, but I would just sing along and dance along, and then

---

■ **TRIVIA ANSWER** / Answer to question on previous page
8th grade

I begged my Dad to buy the records, or my brother or my sister, and one of them always came through. Then I really begged my Dad to buy me that big sign, when they had uncovered it in Manhattan. Do you remember that sign, Daniel?

Daniel: [Agrees] I sure do.

Linda: I wanted that sign so bad I cried, and dad said it wouldn't fit in our house, much less the family car!

Daniel: [Bursts out laughing]

Linda: That was his way of getting out of it.

Daniel: Well, he had the perfect excuse. If it's too big for the trunk, it's *not* coming home [Laughing]! I guess that would explain why you never got that pony you had always wanted, right?

Linda: Aha, after all these years I can now finally figure it out [Laughing]. …So, what he did was buy me an album instead. And he had his own private stereo, and I was only allowed to play it when I played Elvis.

Daniel: Got ya, …that's very good.

Linda: It was wonderful.

Daniel: What about you Richard?

Richard: Okay, I started, …well, I didn't really get to into Elvis until I met Linda. As you know, I was born in the late or mid 40's and grew up with the Doo-Wops of the 50's…like singing in hallways and at little corner stores.

Daniel: You sang in hallways?

■ **TRIVIA QUESTION** / View answer on next page

In which family member's car did Elvis take his driver's test?

Richard: Yeah, singing to get an echo [Laughing].

Daniel: [Laughing] You were probably the type of kid that put his head between the speakers and thought he was in a recording studio!

Richard: This is true [Both laughing].

Daniel: Richard, you are not alone. As a kid, I also put my head in between speakers imagining myself to be in the studio cutting a record with a tape recorder going right under my chin! If it weren't for all those noises in the house, like having my mother vacuuming or kids screaming outside, it sure would have been a great recording session! Matter of fact, I got into it so deep that we almost got kicked out of the building because the music was *sooo* loud! Richard, only difference in our speaker studios is that I did not sing. Seriously, Richard and Linda, I cannot sing! The other day I felt like singing a little and killed all the plant life in my house!

Richard and Linda: [Laughing] You're a real clown [Laughing]!

Richard: So, I was really into Doo-Wop, especially since I played ball with Dion and some of the Belmonts and the Regents. Every so often I would also sing with Barbara Ann. Ernie Maresca is also a friend; he was a songwriter and a singer. So back then, around the Bronx, you could find a lot of groups singing, so it was only normal that I was really into Doo-Wop, and then I met Linda [Laughing].

She was always telling me about Elvis, Elvis, Elvis, and I said, "Elvis who"? I was trying to figure out what Doo-Wop singer Elvis was supposed to be.

Daniel: [Laughing]

■ **TRIVIA ANSWER** / Answer to question on previous page
He took the test in his uncle Travis's 1940 Buick.

Richard: I saw him on Steve Allen singing to some basset hound, and I said, "What [Laughing]?" And, then he was on the Sinatra show, and I thought, "So, this guy has to be somebody or have something." I really started to get into Elvis when I met Linda; she was such a fan of his that I listened to all of his music with her. I got around to really liking him and following his career from the 60's when Linda and I were first together.

Daniel: Okay, anything to add to that Linda?

Linda: Ah, well, it wasn't too hard to convince Richard that Elvis was the King. He listened to his music, he looked at some of his films, and he knew that Elvis was handsome and dynamic as a singer and that Elvis was so very generous!

Richard didn't know anything about his background, like how he contributed to St. Jude's and many charities, so that helped to inspire Richard to become a fan immediately. It really did not take a lot of convincing him.

Richard: I remember when we spent all night with our little son at Madison Square Garden, when he first appeared in New York. Daniel, you know, I wasn't like some fans that were literally eight years old when they first heard of Elvis, but I will never forget all those fans when that man walked out on the stage. It was like God was all of a sudden appearing on that stage! I mean, they were either screaming or crying in total awe. I mean I'm sitting in the audience saying, "I don't believe he has affected all these people in all these different ways, all at the same time."

■**TRIVIA QUESTION** / View answer on next page
Which two former employees of Memphis radio station WREC played a tremendous part in Elvis's career?

Elvis just walked out after "2001 Space Odyssey" stopped playing (with Ronnie Tutt on drums), and you heard that beat of the drums and Elvis's band. He walked out wearing all white, and I said, "Oh My God, what is this?"

Daniel: [Chuckles]

Richard: I said, "What is happening?"

Linda: And you had seen him in Las Vegas.

Richard: I had seen him there, sure; but, you know, Las Vegas is really glitzy, with all those movie stars and sneakin' in the back, you know, with Sinatra and Sammy Davis, Jr., and all this kinda stuff. But, in Madison Square Garden in New York—that is my home turf in New York— when Elvis walked out, I couldn't believe how he affected something like 20,000 people at the Garden. It was just unbelievable! I will never, ever, forget that day, ever!

Daniel: Well, why don't I ask you this question, because we're gonna start putting the zoom lens on when you saw Elvis in Vegas, as well. Before that, what you were probably describing was an opening night. But, what I'd like to ask both of you is: As you knew you were going to Madison Square Garden, when did you know you were getting tickets? Give me all of your feelings and emotions and experiences that led up to the actual show, you know, like the day of the show, and the excitement building, talking about going to the Elvis show with other co-workers, the ticket lines, people with the bedrolls, and all that stuff. Give me a zoom lens on that so we can truly capture that moment for all of the readers that have only heard about this. What was it like for you leading up to the big show...and don't worry about who is going to say what [Laughing].

■ **TRIVIA ANSWER** / Answer to question on previous page
Sam Phillips and Marion Keisker.

I'm gonna ask both of you, so you can bounce off each other while you reminisce about what you both experienced individually; so I'm gonna give you the floor now.

Richard: Yeah, Linda told me that when we saw him in Vegas, it was announced that Elvis was gonna appear in New York, which was so far out of the realm of our reality. I said, "Yeah, okay, sure, Elvis is coming to The Big Apple." So, as soon as we knew he was gonna be at Madison Square Garden, we knew we had to get down there to get tickets the moment they would go on sale. Since we did not have a babysitter, we had to take our young son. I can still remember the hallway we were waiting in.

Linda: It was outside.

Richard: Yeah, it was the outside hallway at Madison Square Garden before you got into the ticket center, which was enclosed and locked up for the night. So, we stood outside in this huge line in the middle of the night with their security guards walking back and forth. Our son slept, thank God, most of the night on a…

Linda: Blanket

Richard: Yeah, on a blanket, and when we got right up to the ticket window, we got seats in a loge, which was like, unfortunately, far away from the stage, not the loge closest to the stage. The scalpers were, of course, buying up the tickets so quickly. There was no seating arrangement chart to show us, so when we got up to the window, I just said to the ticket agent, "Give me the closest seats you have," and he said, "Well, I think the only thing I have is like the 20th or 30th row."

■TRIVIA QUESTION / View answer on next page
Which one of Elvis's family members at one time worked at Britling's Cafeteria and at St. Joseph's Hospital as a nurse's aide?

I said, "Oh my gosh, that's so far back, how 'bout loge?" And he goes, "We have loge," but it was the wrong loge—the one at the rear of the Garden's stadium instead of the main one at the front of the Garden. So, we came away really disappointed that we got such lousy seats after waiting all night long.

Linda: There were about 100 people ahead of us in line!

Richard: Exactly. That happened because the scalpers in line were buying tickets up so quickly that we never had a chance at the good seats! We did not find this out until after we got to our seats; and, being that far back, Elvis would've been nothing more than a memory! That's when Linda said, "I'm gonna write a letter, or I'm gonna make a phone call," and I knew then that I was gonna turn this over to her 'cause she did this all on her own. I'm gonna let her tell about experiences with Jerry Weintraub and what a great guy he turned out to be!

Daniel: Okay.

Linda: What happened was, I was devastated that I didn't have a seat where I could really see his face, and, of course, I wasn't going to stand for that! So, I wrote a letter, sending it along with a picture of myself, to Jerry Weintraub explaining that my son slept on the floor with us all night just to get lousy "wrong loge" seats. And I also let him know how upset I was. Within a couple of days, our home phone rang [Of course, I'd included the number in my letter to him]. It was a representative of the entourage in Jerry's office, offering me tickets to every Elvis concert on the tour!

Daniel: *WOW!*

■ **TRIVIA ANSWER** / Answer to question on previous page

Gladys Presley

Linda: This time the seats were magnificent. ...It was amazing...on the floor, second row, seventh row. And, Richard had to sit up in the bleachers, because I took my son with me close up to Elvis. He even told Elvis that "Mommy loves you", and then Elvis said, "I love her too, and I want her to come up to the stage for a scarf," but my son was so young, he was frightened, and he didn't want to go, so I said, "That's okay. I just had the most magnificent seats. On occasion, I would call Jerry, and he would take my calls, and it really just opened a lot of doors. I was actually invited to attend the press conference. We got picked up in a limousine and were invited to be one of the only non-press people included! But, unfortunately, my husband had an emergency at work that night, so it never happened.

Daniel: Ohhh...

Linda: So, I was really sad about that.

Daniel: Linda, that was a famous press conference.

Linda: Yes it was, and I was going to be right there, talking to him and seeing him, and it was really great that Jerry Weintraub offered me such a marvelous opportunity! But, I just couldn't make it. I did, however, go to all the concerts, and then they invited me to tour with Elvis for three months as part of the entourage! But, my son was still a baby, and I couldn't leave him.

Daniel: Linda, what did Richard have to say about you being invited to go on tour and everything? Richard, where were you [All laughing]?

Richard: First of all, I was shocked by the offer, dumbfounded, actually.

■ **TRIVIA QUESTION** / View answer on next page

When Elvis played guitar in the Humes High Band, how did the Annual Minstrel spell his name on the evening program of April 9, 1953?

Then when I had a moment to collect my thoughts, I said, "Well I gotta go to work. Are you gonna leave Richard with Mom and Dad, because we don't have a babysitter, you know. ....I want you to think about this because it's an amazing offer to be able to go on tour with the King of Rock 'n' Roll. *But*, you have just got to think that we have a young son, and I have to leave him all day long to go to my job and earn money. What are we gonna, how are we gonna, work this out? Three months is not three days!"

Daniel: Right, sure.

Richard: I mean we really wracked our brains about this, because she wanted to go so badly, and I kinda wanted her to go because of her missing the press conference. But when reality sets in, you start thinking of everything all at once. You think, "What are you gonna do, especially with a young child— leave him with Mom and Dad while I go to work? Who's gonna feed him, what if he gets sick, where is Linda gonna be, and how then do I reach her if I need her?"

Linda: Richard was really worried about me going off for three months.

Daniel: [Laughing]…with Elvis [Laughing]! Why shouldn't he be worried?

[All laughing]

Richard: Yeah, I mean this is Elvis Presley; this is not some slob off the street. He is the man, the hero of millions and most likely God's gift to women. Think about it…his appeal was so strong that these women would have gladly thrown themselves under a bus, if he had asked them to. What's there not to worry about [Laughing]?

■ **TRIVIA ANSWER** / Answer to question on previous page
  Elvis Prestly

Daniel: Right [Laughing]

Linda: I was *that* close, Daniel!

Richard: I mean, we were in Vegas, and Elvis reached over to shake her hand, and I was *pushing* her to shake his hand.

Linda: But I froze!

Richard: And she couldn't move! I'm lookin' at her saying, "He wants ya; he is standing here, the King of Rock 'n' Roll, in the middle of the Las Vegas Hilton, leaning over the stage to shake your hand, and you're sitting here like, "Ah, ah, ah, I can't move…I won't touch him!" I'm saying, "What the hell is going on?" I'm pushing her, and she's pushing back like I've got to get away from him, and I'm saying I would have dragged him onto the table.

[Daniel and Linda hysterically laughing in the background]

Richard: Elvis is just standing there! I mean, he just stood there and laughed.

Linda: He shook your hand instead, Richard!

Richard: Yeah, he shook my hand. Daniel, would you believe that she wouldn't talk to me because he shook my hand! I kept showing her the hand and saying, "I'm gonna wash…say good-bye to Elvis!" Oh, man, I had a lot of fun with that for a long time!

Daniel: I am sure you did, Richard [Laughing].

Richard: I can still see Elvis standing there smiling and walking away…

■ **TRIVIA QUESTION** / View answer on next page
Where did Dixie Locke notice Elvis for the first time?

Linda: Then he walked back and sang a song to all of us at the table. But I was just in shock since I've never been in that type of situation before.

Daniel: [Laughing] Neither had anybody else at your table!

Linda: At least they were smart enough to shake his hand and reach out even though I didn't.

Daniel: Well, you know, you did something none of them have done... you didn't shake Elvis's hand, but you were allowed to [Laughing]!

Linda: I'm still mad at Richard!

Daniel: Well, don't be mad at him. It's not his fault; he was actually trying to get you to shake the hand when you locked up on him like a Nevada burro!

Linda: I did. I *really* did.

Daniel: Well, Linda, there's not much you can do about changing the past, ya know?

Richard: Linda has been presented with so many opportunities that are incredible. Let me tell you about the time when we were in Philadelphia, outside in the freezing rain with no tickets. A guard appeared out of the clear blue sky, and he stood there to ask us if we wanted to come down next to the stage and watch Elvis's concert.

Linda: That guard really did that.

Richard: Daniel, this guy didn't know us from Adam. I mean, I just looked at Linda and said, "Look at some of the opportunities that were open to you."

■ **TRIVIA ANSWER** / Answer to question on previous page
During a church function.

Daniel: This is obviously no longer a fluke. Linda's gotta be amazing looking in order for everybody to unroll like a rug.

Linda: [Laughing] not really!

Richard: It's just her magic; there's just something about Linda that… I don't know…guards open up doors. I mean you want to come and see Elvis at the Hilton? She was invited up to his floor to watch him play ball in the hallway. These things actually happened to Linda, and I'd just stand back and watch and say, "Oh my God, I don't believe this," because it is so unbelievable! Nobody would ever believe it. It's really amazing; the doors open up…and the other things that happen to her, like when Elvis was anywhere around or in the vicinity. You know, even watching him come out of the car at 3 am in New York.

Daniel: Let's talk about that for a second. Linda why don't you pick up the ball from there and tell the readers what happened when the car pulled up in New York.

Linda: Daniel, oh my goodness, wow, this was after we saw him in Las Vegas! I had a guard stop me, because he saw me in line every single day for all of the concerts, and he said to me, "If you'll meet me here at midnight, I will take you to his 'After Party,'" and I was just so thrilled! But my husband, Richard, was *not!*"

Daniel: Of course not.

Linda: He said, "I'm not going to let you go. …Was I invited?" And I said, "No, you weren't."

Daniel: I guess that settled that [Laughing].

■ **TRIVIA QUESTION** / View answer on next page

When Elvis first met the Jordanaires, who were they singing backup for?

Linda: And, he didn't let me go. So you *know*, I was not *happy*.

Daniel: [Laughs] How can you blame him, Linda [Laughing]? Can you just imagine how loud it would have been in your house if you had gone?

Linda: Pretty loud [Laughing]! We found which hotel he was going to be staying at and when he was going to be arriving. So, at 3 am he pulled up in the limo and just got out, took off his dark sunglasses, started laughing, and said, "What are you guys doing out here at this hour?" He was just so friendly; he shook our hands, and some of the girls ran up and kissed him. I did not but just watched him, and I said, "Oh, you actually walk, talk and breathe!"

Daniel: [Laughing] Did you think he was a stuffed bear?

Linda: He was real and in the flesh right in front of me, and Rich just laughed. I was shocked that he actually walked into the hotel himself. I would have bet that Elvis would actually have had somebody carry him into the hotel on one of those beds the Roman Emperors used to lay on [Laughter] or something! He was so human and down to earth.

Richard: He really was, like when he spotted the fans, even after his bodyguards were rushing him into this little alcove that had an elevator up to the Penthouse. He actually stopped them from rushing him along, and he turned around and was really very personable. He was smiling, although, God knows that he was probably tired as hell, especially at 3 o'clock in the morning. He just wanted to stay with us and to talk like a normal person, not like the King of Rock 'n' Roll. He had just wanted to be one of the guys and shoot the breeze for a little while!

■ **TRIVIA ANSWER** / Answer to question on previous page
Eddy Arnold

Linda: He was not exactly sprinting to get away.

Richard: He just wanted to say, "Hi!" He wanted to know about who we were…something like, "Who are you?…Where are you from…?" kind of thing, you know? I am sure the guards were saying "Ah, no Elvis, we don't know who these people are; this is an uncontrolled environment; let's get you into the elevator so we can know you're safe and get you back up to your room." They did it very well, very smooth.

Linda: Yes very loose and casual.

Richard: Even though it was very early in the morning and we were all dog-assed tired, he walks up and makes you feel like you're alive. There was something about him…magic…like I said, with Linda. You just feel like you're alive; you don't care what time of the morning it is or if it's cold or if it's rainy. You know, this is Elvis Presley.

You know, you just have to stop and look at him.

Linda: I talked to him then; I said, "Elvis, you look tired," and he said, "I am, honey [Chuckling]."

Daniel: See, you finally got your mouth to open and words to come out [Laughing]!

Linda: I did, I tell ya, I figured that it was about time I say something instead of just staring at him in awe again. He was just so pleasant to everyone.

Daniel: [Laughing] But, it's too bad he didn't remember you from the stage—the lady that froze up!

Linda: [Laughing] Thank God, he didn't!

■ TRIVIA QUESTION / View answer on next page
What was the result after Houston DJ Biff Collie saw Elvis at the Eagles Nest?

Daniel: Nassau Coliseum, Richard, what do you remember about that particular performance?

Linda: Oh, the fan clubs were there!

Richard: Yes, the fan clubs were there. I don't remember where our seats were.

Linda: We had pretty close seats.

Richard: Pretty close seats yeah; we had three seats together. We sat there, and I remember the anxiety after we were getting there, parking the car, running up. Even though we had tickets, we were following all these people into various entrances or exits that were available leading to the Arena. So, just the challenge of finding out where our seats were, plus having to deal with what was it, a comic or something like that...

Linda: That was a shame. Richard, please tell Daniel about what, in both places, happened to the comedians.

Richard: I'm sitting there saying, "I am in the middle of something I can't explain!"

Then, a light hits the curtain and, all of a sudden, out comes Elvis onto the stage, wearing white! I mean it just takes your breath away. You absolutely lose your breath; you're just like...aaah! You just look at him, you can't breathe, and you can't move. He's up there; you just see this man, and oh my, the feelings that are going through you! I see my wife—she's screaming, crying, jumping, and our son is saying, "What's going on with Mom?" You know, [Linda laughing in background] I'm like, look at the people. You've an adrenaline rush going through you,

Wise men say only fools rush in
But I can't help falling in love with you
Shall I stay
Would it be a sin
If I can't help falling in love with you

and you're kinda like just in awe. You are carried along for the next 45 minutes, and you don't want the ride to stop. You don't want him to sing "I Can't Help Falling in Love", because you know it's the end.

Daniel: Right.

Richard: That's when you know he's leaving.

Linda: And, everybody cries.

Richard: You see people rushing the stage and being pushed back by security.

You see Elvis walking along the stage edge singing, and you are being carried along as a river current. It's like a ride at Disneyland; you do not want it to end, but you know it's going too far too soon! And you can't wait for the next time you're going to see him, and you get all these

■TRIVIA QUESTION / View answer on next page
During the '69 Press Conference Elvis wore a scarf. What were the three colors of this scarf?
(Hint: can be found on our web site tcbjoe.com)

diverse feeling inside you. It's so hard to explain it to somebody that's never seen it before all live. Because I always ask people, "Oh, I'm an Elvis fan…have you ever seen him perform live? I am not talking about TV; I'm not talking about his movies. Have you ever seen him perform *LIVE*-in-person? Because if you haven't, you don't know what it is to be in the shadow of a superstar…a man who could take you away from your bills, your in-law problems and your work problems, and for 45 minutes hold you in the palm of his hands." Then, he would just sing like you were the only person in that stadium. That's the way that each and all of those 20,000 people in the Nassau Coliseum felt, the same way he affected everyone at Madison Square Garden. I cannot explain to anybody the feeling, that euphoric feeling of listening to Elvis sing for 45 minutes and banter with Charlie and J.D. Sumner and the Stamps Quartet.

Linda: And the Sweet Inspirations.

Richard: There's no way to describe the feeling of seeing him perform live. There's no way. There just are no words, because of the feelings you experience, and you can't describe the feelings to anybody. I can look at you and say, "Oh, okay." I don't know what else to say, Daniel…you just can't describe it; I can't put it into words.

Linda: And he's a late fan. You can imagine how I felt—I was in heaven.

Daniel: I am sure you were, Linda [Laughing].

Linda: I told Richard all I have to do is *look* at him; he doesn't even have to *say* a word—just stand there and let me look at him, and I am happy.

■ **TRIVIA ANSWER** / Answer to question on previous page
Red, black and white

Daniel: [Laughing happily]

Linda: Unfortunately, what we also recall from this performance, as well as the one at Madison Square Garden, is how badly the fans treated those comics. When those entertainers came out, nobody wanted to hear them. We wanted Elvis. Every one of his fans, the fan clubs and all the people there ranted, "Elvis! Elvis! Elvis!" All of us were just screaming, "Bring him on, bring Elvis on!"

Daniel: Right.

Linda: As if by magic, everyone settled down and let the comic continue, because that's what Elvis wanted us to do; so we did it respectfully!

Daniel: Jackie Kahane was a good guy and a great comedian.

Linda: Yeah, but he got rotten treatment from people who were just waiting on the edge of their seats for Elvis to start his performance.

Daniel: Jackie did mention that one time. …You have to understand something…when Elvis is in the house everyone, and I mean everyone, takes the number two slot. You just don't have a chance to stand out. He was *that* big!

Richard: Yeah, I can imagine, and I'm sure that was not the only time that happened to him, especially when you are trying to lighten the mood of an audience to get ready for Elvis.

Linda: I felt really bad for him after awhile 'cause some people were really rude. And I mean rude, Daniel. That's when Elvis said, "No, you are treating him badly, and *that* is hurting me." When we heard that, we knew we had to accept the comedian and treat him kindly!

■ **TRIVIA QUESTION** / View answer on next page
What was the nickname for Hank Garland, and what role did he play in Elvis's life?

Daniel: That's right.

Richard: Daniel, I was one of the people who organized the vigil for Elvis after he passed. We had tickets to the Nassau Coliseum, which we still have, and we never turned them in to get our money back. I know that when we got word that he had passed away, one of the guys from New York said, "What are you gonna do about the concert at the Nassau Coliseum that we all have tickets for?" And I said, "I'm gonna go." He looked at me and said, "Go for what?" I said, "I have nothing else to do. I don't have any other place to be. I need to be where Elvis was gonna be. I'm gonna go to the Nassau Coliseum and just stand in an empty parking lot, hold my ticket in my hand, and I'm gonna cry."

Linda: Thousands showed up there.

Richard: It turned out that one guy heard me and said, "Oh, I'm gonna come there with you if you don't mind. I'll bring my projector and my films."

Linda: And, I'll bring the music and tapes.

Richard: And I said, "Sure, I'm gonna be there anyway." I told Linda, "There's nowhere else on earth I'd rather be."

Daniel: Where else would you want to be? I mean your whole heart is there. All you would be able to think about is where you should be.

Richard: Exactly!

Daniel: It's like, there's nothing else; there's nothing else to do. And, there is nothing else to top that when it is your life.

■ **TRIVIA ANSWER** / Answer to question on previous page
Sugarfoot. He was a guitar player for Elvis.

Richard: I didn't want to do anything else but stand in that empty parking lot. I didn't care if I was there all alone. I'm gonna stand here, where I know he was gonna be on stage, and look at my watch and say, "He's appearing right now." (in my mind and heart)…Then "2001" has just ended, and Elvis is then on his way entering the stage, and I could see the light hitting that curtain. I am gonna stand here for the next 45 minutes, and I'm gonna cry. …I will be staying right here; I am not gonna go anywhere.

Linda: There were thousands of people that showed up because word had gotten out to the radio stations about what we were doing.

Richard: The radio stations were there…the TV stations. I said in my head when I hear "I Can't Help Falling in Love" then [Choking up] and only then, am I gonna get back into my car and come back to my life of bills and of in-laws and everything else that's bugging me— work and what not—but, for that hour, I'm gonna, excuse me, be like Elvis *never* left "the building"…or us. He's still here; maybe we are just waiting outside that building, waiting for the limo to come out of the underground parking garage with Elvis and Joe Esposito in the back seat. I just had to re-live it just one more time, and that is what I did. I was one of the two people that started the Nassau Coliseum vigil.

Linda: A tribute to him.

Richard: A tribute to him, and we were there, and we were exchanging memories and stories and crying. That's what we did.

Daniel: Let me ask you a question: When you found out that, ah, Elvis passed away, can you tell me, starting with Linda, where you were when you heard the news?

■ **TRIVIA QUESTION** / View answer on next page
How much money did 20th Century Fox pay Elvis for making the movie *Love Me Tender*?

Linda: Yes I can tell you exactly. I was going to give my son a bath, and happened to go into the room that had the TV on. …They flashed across the screen a bulletin, and I let out such a scream which caused my little son to come running, very scared asking, "Mommy, what's the matter?" I just continued to scream and cry, and I said, "No, this isn't right, this isn't true. This can't be; they're making a mistake." My son was just standing there with his robe on 'cuz I forgot about the bath. He knew Mommy was very upset. All I did was continue to be hysterical saying, "They've made a mistake, this just can't be!" So, when Richard came home—he didn't know, because he had to travel on a bus from Manhattan. When he walked in the door he saw me sobbing in the corner on the couch and my son sitting next to me. He said, "What is wrong, what happened?" When I told him he couldn't believe it either. He broke down, and then my family started to call on the phone because they knew how I was affected, and they wanted to know if I was okay. It was a terrible moment in my life, one that my son still remembers. He said, "Mom, I'll never forget you. I've never, ever, seen you so upset."

Daniel: Richard, let's give Linda a moment. What are your thoughts?

Richard: I was coming home from Manhattan; I had to take a special express bus since it cut around all the traffic. I got on the bus from work, and I still didn't know what was going on, you know. So, I was walking up midtown Manhattan, and nobody was talking about anything that I heard. I wasn't given an inkling of what to expect when I got home. Before I got off the bus, about a half a block from my house, I had noticed our house was dark. As I'm walking up to it, I'm saying, "There are no lights on…maybe she left…maybe she went out shopping."

■ **TRIVIA ANSWER** / Answer to question on previous page
$100,000

I don't know what's going on... so, I opened the front door, and I walked in, and there's this little light on, and I see Linda in the corner of the couch. The whole house is dark except for this little light, which I could not see from the street because the curtains had been closed. I was thinking, "This is not good; I don't know what it is, but it's not good." I said, "Hon, what's going on?" And, she goes, "Elvis passed away." I said, "No *way!*" And she goes, "Elvis has passed away…he died… he's dead…he's gone…no more Elvis."

I said, "It can't be. Elvis is gonna live forever, he's immortal. How can he pass away?" Of course the TV was on, and there was a picture of him outlined in black, and the phone is ringing, and all I can hear is this phone ringing. It seemed to keep ringing forever and I said, "Hon, do you want me to answer it?" She said, "No, don't answer that phone. I don't want to talk to anybody." So, after the second or third time, the phone started ringing again. I picked it up, and it was her sister saying, "How's Linda?" I just got home, and I'm in shock. I don't know what to do…I can't comfort her…I mean the King of Rock 'n' Roll is gone! I'm never gonna see him again…he is dead…it's not true! I have tickets to see his concert… *NO! NO! NO!* How could this happen?" You know, *how could he leave us?* This is what I thought…how could he leave us? He was so much a part of my life; it was like a family member leaving.

How could he leave us? We need him. We need him to make us happy, to make us sing, to put a song in our heart or a smile on our face. How could he leave us? It's not fair. We needed him to complete our lives.

Linda: Sometimes he gave us our only smile.

■ **TRIVIA QUESTION** / View answer on next page
Which Memphis television station did Elvis appear on to promote traffic safety and driver education?

Richard: I kept thinking, "What's going on…why is God doing this?" And it was just the most unbelievable haunting evening. I never, ever, want to go through that again.

Linda: And the next three days…

Richard: The next three days we were trying to make our arrangements to go to Memphis. All the flights were booked going into Memphis; we just couldn't get a flight out, and I told Linda that we were gonna get down there, sooner or later, to walk the grounds. And after they had, ah, moved him to Graceland into the garden with his mom, we were finally able to get a flight down to Memphis and walk up the driveway and to the Meditation Garden to see and take pictures of his tombstone; and, I don't know, that day is burned into my memory, because losing Elvis was like losing a family member, someone that made you feel great when you were not feeling great, someone who made you sing when you didn't feel like singing.

Elvis humbly did all of those things for countless thousands of people. I'm sure he did it to all of his fans, and losing him was one of the worst losses.

Linda: I did lose part of my family and some of my soul when he died.

Daniel: [Clears his throat]

Richard: There was no recovering from it, just no recovering—no relief. The pain hit you deep in your gut. Daniel, that event hurt to the core.

Linda: Even to this day.

Daniel: What do you remember when you saw the funeral procession…and when you saw the white hearse on TV?

Linda: My heart was broken, Daniel, it really was. I could not stand to see it. When I watched it, I sobbed and sobbed. To this day, anytime it…I have different films and they show that, or I look at my memorial books, and I see that I am still brought to tears each time…it just couldn't be. It was like watching an angel who had been brought here right after World War II to give the world a healing it desperately needed…and then watching this event marking the end…that was really too much to handle. I couldn't accept it or believe it.

Richard: That white car brought me to my knees [Voice lowered].

Linda: That white hearse…watching it driving down the street was one of the hardest things to see. Daniel, I had lost my mother the year before Elvis died and, quite honestly, I don't think I cried as hard then as I did when Elvis died.

My mom was very ill and suffered a lot, yet when she was put out of all her suffering, I really thanked God for that. But, the shock of Elvis dying the very next year put me in a pretty dark and bad place. It was very sad.

Richard: Yeah, that funeral procession was difficult to watch. They had a special midnight showing of *Elvis On Tour* in some little remote theatre out on Long Island in New York. So Linda and I went to it because they were gonna show it at midnight, and I knew they were showing the Monty Python something, and they had all these young kids that were into Monty Python. Then they showed *Elvis On Tour*,

■ **TRIVIA QUESTION** / View answer on next page
What occupation did Penny Banner have when she was involved with Elvis?

and we sat through that movie. When the lights went up in the theatre, we were all sitting there with tears running down our face. Linda said, "We never moved, because I remembered him in the backseat with Joe Esposito just looking out the window…that gorgeous face" So, I fought back these memories of Elvis so naturally and earnestly waving to me, of shaking my hand, of waiting all night long together at Madison Square Garden. So, really, we were sitting in our seats crying. These young kids were looking at us like, "What the hell's wrong with these old people?" You know like, "What are they crying for?" We were frozen in our seats and just could not move.

When we finally walked out of the theatre, there were tears running down our faces. It was…I mean…we just could not get over the fact that he was gone. We just couldn't get over the fact that God took him from us at such an early age.

Daniel: Yes, it is pretty sad. Richard, let me ask both of you the following question: What message would you like to send to the next generation Elvis fans out there? Ladies first.

Linda: *Oh*! Listen to his music, watch his films, get to know him, and get to know his voice, and you will be a fan forever. No doubt about it!

Daniel: Richard?

Richard: There will never be…there will never be…let me repeat myself, if you can put it in capital letters…the generation of TODAY, there will NEVER, EVER be another ELVIS PRESLEY! He really had a God-given talent, and he humbly used it to entertain people. Elvis did not use it to hurt people, and he wasn't selfish.

■ **TRIVIA ANSWER** / Answer to question on previous page

She was a female wrestler.

Linda: And, Elvis was so generous!

Richard: With the talents that God gave him…just listen to his music. I know he's been gone 30 years, but look at his films and see the way he interacted with his fans…

Linda: And keep his memory alive!!!

Richard: Elvis just made them feel special; he made them feel like he was only singing to them. Enjoy his music, respect his talent. And I really feel sorry for the generations coming that never will have the privilege and opportunity to actually see Elvis perform live, like we did. We were blessed by God to be able to see him live several times. People will never be able to see that again…the hysteria…the excitement. There has been nothing like it since. Losing Elvis is a huge loss that we still feel. But enjoy what he left us; he left us his music, his pictures…

Linda: And the books describing his life.

Richard: Enjoy the rich legacy Elvis has left us: his voice, his music, his records and his movies.

Daniel: Ladies and Gentleman, Linda and Richard Albanese. ♦

Did You Know?

That Elvis, Scotty and Bill had stayed at the Captain Shreve Hotel when they arrived in Shreveport, Louisiana, to try out for Louisiana Hayride. ♦

■ **TRIVIA QUESTION** / View answer on next page
Where did Elvis have his last public performance before going into the Army?

Up Close and Personal:
The Imperials

A candid conversation between Joe Esposito and Daniel Lombardy

Daniel: What do you remember about working with the Imperials?

Joe: Well, we used to work with them during a lot of recording sessions. That is how Elvis first got on to them. Sometimes, if J.D Sumner was not available, they would bring in the Imperials. As you know, in the early days, J.D and the Stamps Quartet traveled a lot. We all knew that the Imperials were a great gospel group. They were a bunch of young guys, and Joe Moscheo managed their group.

Joe was the guy with the sideburns, seen in That's The Way It Is when they were harmonizing without Elvis, in the room?

Yeah, Joe is the dark Italian guy with the sideburns.

He almost looked like he was trying to be Elvis.

[Laughing]…what can I tell you [Laughing], but anyway, they were a bunch of good guys, a really good group, and Elvis liked them. You know how much he had loved gospel groups.

Is there anything else that stands out in your memory about the Imperials? Did they ever hang out with Elvis, you know, like when he was touring?

A lot of times, they would visit upstairs at our suite. It was, like I said, many times over the years. Elvis really liked to sit up there and sing gospel music 'til all hours! They would come up, not just to sing, but also to hang out and meet up with a few of the ladies [Laughing].

■ **TRIVIA ANSWER** / Answer to question on previous page
Schofield Barracks, Pearl Harbor, Hawaii.

Right, I got you [Laughing].

[Laughing]

Ahhh, the spoils of the job…[Laughing harder].

[Laughing] Yep, that's it! ♦

Up Close and Personal: Elvis and Slot cars

A candid conversation between Joe Esposito and Daniel Lombardy

Daniel: At one time, Elvis was pretty heavy into slot cars. What do you remember about that time?

Joe: Well, if you recall back in the sixties, slot cars were really hot items. They used to have all these places with slot cars and tracks, and all that, where you could rent them. Well, we used to go to this one place not too far from Graceland, just a short ways down the street. We would often go over there to rent it out late at night, after they closed.

Uh huh.

After renting the place for a while, Elvis finally said, "Okay, guys, we have to get our own slot cars, alright?" So, we went out, and he bought us each the slot cars that we wanted. After playing with them for a while, he said, "Shit, I gotta have one of these tracks!" I was surprised and answered, "Really?" so Elvis said, "Yeah!" Daniel, do you know where the Trophy Room at Graceland is now? That was originally built for our slot cars!

■ **TRIVIA QUESTION** / View answer on next page
Where was Colonel Parker located when Elvis delivered him a red Isetta sports car for his birthday?

Oh, wow!

There was a big patio overlooking Elvis's pool at Graceland…so what he did was to make this huge room for our use, because the slot car tracks were really big!

Right.

I mean they were huge! So, Elvis had that built for us, to have a slot car track put in there. We used to spend hours and hours in there, racing each other around on the slot car tracks "inside" this house. And, sure, he really got into that, but you know, that's Elvis. He would go all out in this…he rides and drives and crashed them, and that destroyed them! Then, after a while, Elvis would just get tired of it.

Did you guys ever get into any heated debates? Because I know that, when you slot car race, it can get really competitive…people can easily lose their tempers and get into really serious arguments, resulting in people waking up in hospitals after getting knocked out [Laughing]!

[Laughing] No, we never got serious in that way; we just had fun with it!

You know, one car would crash; then we would just die laughing, going, "Did you see that one fly out?" Elvis did not get into it seriously; he just enjoyed what he was doing 'cause it was a lot of fun. It was just a big social event for all of us. You know, it was like everything that Elvis ever did in his life. He over killed on it or got tired of it, and then he never did it again!

[Laughing] how long did the slot car period last?

Oh, I remember that it lasted about a year to a year and an half.

That's a long time [Laughing].

Yep. I mean it was there for a year and a half; but, we didn't use it during that whole time, you know what I'm saying?

I sure do. So, you just took the tracks out of there after awhile?

Yeah, they gave it all away, and then Elvis decided to make a Trophy Room out of it. ♦

Fan Spotlight Interview

With Mark Gagnon

Daniel Lombardy: Why don't you tell the readers a little bit about yourself and what got you into Elvis.

Mark Gagnon: Well, let me see. I have always been a pretty big Elvis fan. I have an older sister who was always listening to Elvis music and buying all his record albums. One of my favorite movies, *It Happened at the World's Fair*, means a lot to me because I always wanted to be Kurt Russell so bad!

[Laughing]

You know it's kind of odd that I didn't want to be Elvis, but instead, I wanted to be Kurt Russell [Both laughing].

Mark, perhaps the only reason you probably wanted to do that was so you could say you are the only one to have lived after having

kicked Elvis Presley in the shin!

[Both laughing]

I wanted to be Kurt Russell, because I wanted to be in a movie with Elvis.

Right.

Because there weren't any other movies ever coming out having child actors in them, you know…and those twins who had appeared in *Follow That Dream*…

[Agreeing]

[Laughing]

So when you were a kid you said, "Hey, man, I wish that were me!"

Yeah!

I gotcha.

And then I thought he was the epitome of cool…just so, so cool on screen. It was just everything he did. It was just so cool. I was thinking, "Is this just the right thing to do, the right place to be, or what?" It was just that cool. Elvis was really the ultimate cool person. He was just that cool.

What are you talking about? Elvis was the Duke of Cool, man!

[Laughing] That's the word I was looking for [Laughing].

[Still laughing].

■ **TRIVIA ANSWER** / Answer to question on previous page
Michael Curtiz

Elvis died when I was 16 years old. In high school, we did a yearly talent show, and that year I got up and sang "Heartbreak Hotel". I had always been a very big fan, but before that time, I had not ever seen anybody else perform that song, other than Elvis! After graduating from high school, I joined the U.S. Army.

What did you do in the Army?

I was a Ranger.

Really?

Yes, an Airborne Ranger.

Which Battalion were you in?

I was in the 1st Battalion, 75th Infantry.

…oh, at Hunter Army Airfield.

Yeah, Hunter Army Airfield. Wow, most civilians would never know that…how do you know that?

We chewed some of the same dirt many moons ago [Smiling].

Small world.

It sure is. Mark, why don't you tell the readers what started your journey into becoming a tribute artist.

In 1994, my team was in Las Vegas doing "Red Flag" at Nellis Air Force Base. You remember "Red Flag" don't you?

I sure do.

■ **TRIVIA QUESTION** / View answer on next page

Which person close to Elvis was allowed to say these words in one of Elvis's movies: "…See you next week, baby"?
(Hint: this was spoken to a prostitute.)

Well, in 1994, as I mentioned, we were stationed near Las Vegas, and anyway, there was a convention going on at Harrah's Casino… so I thought, let me go over there to see what it's all about!

Okay.

But when I went over to the convention and stood in line, I started talking with some people who were ready to go in. All of a sudden an older, heavy-set, gray-haired promoter wearing an Elvis Concert jacket walked by with a frustrated look on his face.

Okay.

So, he sees me out of the corner of his eye. Then he walks over and grabs me by the arm. He asked me, "Where the hell have you been?" So, my reaction was like, "*Whoa, Bud,* I think you've got me confused with somebody else!" So, he keeps trying to start pulling me out of the line [Laughing].

[Laughing hard]

So I pulled him in and got him into an arm lock and said, "Hey, Bud, you have obviously got me confused with someone else…you better let go of me right this instant [Growling]."

Oh hell!

So, he says, "Look guy, let me talk to you." He went on to say, "This event takes 48 Elvises, and there are supposed to be four shows with 12 guys in each. I only have 47 guys! I need you right away." So he was a guy short. So I said, "I have never done anything like this [Laughs]."

[Laughing] What a way to enter the Elvis World! Please go on.

■ **TRIVIA ANSWER** / Answer to question on previous page
Cliff Gleaves

So he says, "Why don't you come backstage with me…you've got a good look…have you ever considered doing anything like this?" So I said, "Well, yeah, sure I have, but it's not a venue I'm familiar with, I mean, performing as Elvis and all."

[Laughing hard]

I haven't done anything quite like this, you know?

This is hilarious, Mark.

Daniel, I really never did anything quite like that, you know. I would sometimes get up at a karaoke bar and make a fool out of myself and sing a little something, but [Laughs] usually in front of friends you tend to drink with.

[Laughing]

So, I go backstage, and he's introducing me to people, and it's just so cool. There's this one guy—I wish I could remember his name. That guy let me borrow his black leather…he was a good guy! And, so the promoter told me that I was going to go on as number seven out of this first group of 12. I'm thinking, man, I don't know…I just got talked into this thing. So, of course, I panic and grab the "courtesy" phone to try reaching my team back at Nellis AFB, as I was thinking, "Come on, you freaking toads, I need you need to get down here [Laughing]."

[Laughing]

I couldn't get through to anybody; so, finally the promoter catches up with me, asking what was I going to sing. Then I started naming songs…. He answers, "No, somebody is already going to sing that one

---

■ **TRIVIA QUESTION** / View answer on next page
Which one of Elvis's cars in Germany was always being driven by Red and Lamar?

in your group." I was thinking then that I needed to see what the others were singing, so that I could make my choices. So, the promoter shows me the list…I give him my three songs…and he is okay with that, you know! So, I'm backstage with a CD player and headphones trying to listen to these songs over and over again.

Sure, sure.

[Laughing] So what happens is that I asked the promoter if there is going to be a screen like in karaoke, a monitor or something, that I can watch the words come up on, or something.

[Laughing]

He says, "Na, man, this is live with a band and orchestra and everything!"

[Laughing really hard]

[Laughing] This is live in front of demanding Elvis fans that are paying to see the show, right?

[Still laughing]

I didn't know that!

This is the real deal!!

So then this promoter starts talking to me, "…you know, man, it's a lot easier with the band. If you mess up, the band just keeps on playin', and then you can just jump right back without looking to bad. But, if you were singing to track music and make a mistake…"

It's unforgivable.

■ **TRIVIA ANSWER** / Answer to question on previous page
The VW "Bug"

That's right! It is because you can't catch right back up, and then you sound like total crap trying to catch up. So I was like, "All right." So he introduces me to the audience and the band as I walk out with black mousse in my hair, and I'm thinking, "Oh man, what the hell am I doing?" I'm getting the sweats, clammy, jelly belly, and all that. So [Laughing], I have no idea what to do—I basically felt like a lost fart in a whirlwind.

[Laughing] Hey, it could have been worse; they could have demanded that you put black shoe polish in your hair [Laughing long and hard]!

Sure they could have at that point. I was so nervous, I could not have told you where I lived under gunpoint!

What a riot!

So, I came out and started to sing "Blue Moon of Kentucky" and then "Follow That Dream" and also "Teddy Bear"…

Okay.

They would only allow you to perform three songs.

I am pretty sure because of the time limitations for each performer, don't you think?

Exactly right! I can still remember not having talked to the audience between songs to build a relationship; so I quickly jumped from song to song [Chuckling], and I did something like, "The next song is 'Follow That Dream'." And then I just jumped into the song "Teddy Bear" right away [Laughing]!

■ **TRIVIA QUESTION** / View answer on next page

Who jokingly mentioned these words to Elvis: "…Your call interrupted my dream of you getting an early Army release; now I don't know how the dream will turn out."?

[Laughing very hard] Listen, Mark, it could have been worse...in your haste, you could have said, "And the next song is 'Follow That Train' [Laughing hard]!"

Yeah, I was like, "Let's finish this thing and get off the damn stage without getting beat up by Aunt Thelma, who has been an Elvis fanatic since the 50's [Laughing]!"

Yep, you have to watch out for her, man; she will put a hurtin' on you. You do a bad show, and you get the stick [Laughing]!

Yeah, I just wanted to finish those songs and get off the stage as quickly as I could, you know? That's pretty much what happened. After the show, people were asking to take pictures with them all over the casino. That was real cool. I was thinking to myself, "Hey man, I can dig this." So when I get back to Nellis, I am telling my team what happened, and they're saying, "Yeah, right, I'll take a pound of what you're havin'… because you be dreamin'!" But, that whole situation was so much fun.

Mark, that was a very unique way to break into becoming a tribute artist.

Yes, I kind of just got thrown to the wolves.

Well, they certainly did not throw you into the pool to see if you could swim. It would appear that they threw you off a cliff to see if you could fly [Laughing]!

[Laughs hard]…pretty much well said, and well put, Daniel.

Mark, what I would like to do at this point is run a scenario by you where a youngster, let's say of 11 years of age, would ask you, "Hey, Mark, I really would like to know who Elvis was. Would you tell me what records and movies you would recommend that would help

me to truly understand Elvis better?" What would your answer be
to the youth?

I would first recommend his earliest of movies, like *Love Me Tender,*
since that is where Elvis had really wanted to break into acting and
everything. He had wanted to be a serious actor. As a song...*Heartbreak
Hotel* and *King Creole*...as Elvis was showing his range. Now all the
other movies were just fluff to me. I mean they were fun movies, where
he's either riding a horse or driving a car or motorcycle or something
else. *The 68 Comeback Special,* where Elvis returns after completing his
movie obligations, is great to watch. Then I would recommend *Elvis On
Tour*...just watch how he progresses; it's amazing and tells a lot about
the person and the performer.

**Tell me a little about the songs you perform onstage. Do you typically
sing mainstream Elvis songs?**

I tend to go for the more obscure songs like "It's Midnight".

It's getting late and
I know that's when I am weak
Funny how things have a way
of looking so much brighter
in the day light
I ought to go to bed
to try and straighten out my head
and just forget you
Oh but it's midnight yes and I miss you

■**TRIVIA QUESTION** / View answer on next page
What role did Dan Robertson play in Elvis's life?

Interesting choice.

Well, it used to be such an obscure song, and it's such a beautiful song. I guess it didn't have a lot of time to hit the mainstream public when it first came out.

What about "Never Fall in Love Again"? Did you ever perform that one?

It's a Tom Jones song, and I have done that song one time. It is one of my wife's favorites. Actually, I have a contest in Charlotte next weekend that is a 2-day event, and I might do that song during the second night… I am definitely going to sing "It's Midnight".

Mark, what message would you like to convey to the new generation Elvis fan out there?

The first thing I would like to mention is that Elvis was such a great humanitarian, and that he was always giving. You know, he came from being poor to rich. No matter how big he eventually became, he always stayed true to America and his fans. Give Elvis a listen, and you will come face to face with a person that will always keep the sun shining on your soul.

What I would like to do at this point is something that we call "Always On My Mind", and we do this all over the world. What I would like you to do is say your name, your location and how Elvis continues to affect and influence your life every day. We are ready to go whenever you are.

Well, gimme a second…you mean now? Or do you want to give me a second?

■ **TRIVIA ANSWER** / Answer to question on previous page
He wrote some of Elvis's most eloquent ballads.

[Laughing] Na, man, its got to be right this instant [Laughing].

[Laughing] Okay.

You got it together now?

Yeah, what do you want me to say again?

[Laughing] Short-term memory loss, huh [Laughing hard]? What I basically would like you to do is say your name and your location and how Elvis continues to influence and affect your life every day. We are ready to roll now [Chuckling]!

This is Mark Gagnon from Fayetteville, North Carolina. I would like to say that Elvis continues to affect my life on a daily basis…damn, what was the rest of that?

[Laughing]…how Elvis continues to influence your life every day.

In my own words or word for word?

No, no [Laughing] no. Just do your own thing, and in your own words [Laughing]. Okay, ready to go—Take 56 [Laughing]! Okay, here you go.

This is Mark Gagnon from Fayetteville, North Carolina, and I'd like to say that…oh balls…what the hell! Shit! I keep forgetting!

Don't worry…we'll cut all that out [Sly grin].

You're going to cut it out?

Sure, sure buddy, no worries [Tilts his head and winks].

This is Mark Gagnon from Fayetteville, North Carolina, and I'd like

---

■ **TRIVIA QUESTION** / View answer on next page
Where was the principle photography for *Roustabout* conducted?

to say that Elvis was a great humanitarian and that he stood for peace and brotherhood in the way that he lived his life and treated people. Throughout his career with his music, especially with the song "If I Can Dream"…that was his message song during the *'68 Comeback Special…* Elvis tried to promote brotherhood, and also with the song titled "Walk a Mile in My Shoes". You don't know a man until you have walked a mile in *his* shoes! ◆

Up Close and Personal: The Stitches of Roustabout

A candid conversation between Joe Esposito and Daniel Lombardy

Daniel: Let's talk about the stitches that Elvis got from performing his own stunts during the filming of Roustabout. Joe, how did that whole thing happen?

Joe: Well, it was in a fight scene, okay? It was during a fight scene that was choreographed and worked out. They were shooting, and what happened was, when this guy fell down, his shoe hit Elvis near his left eye. It cut him right above his eyebrow, and naturally everybody was freaked out when it was lookin' really terrible with blood and all that stuff! So, then they stopped filming, and we all jumped into a car to take Elvis over to the nearest hospital. I think that they gave him eight stitches, and really, it looked a lot worse than it was. Basically, that's what it was. Actually, I will never forget this fact about that movie shoot: Raquel Welch was in the cast when she was just starting to become an actress. She was one of the girls in the "fight" scene.

■ **TRIVIA ANSWER** / Answer to question on previous page
Hidden Valley Ranch north of Los Angeles.

I don't think Elvis would have felt it, for instance, if she had hit him in the head with a shoe [Laughs]!

[Laughs] Also, what I'll never forget...Raquel being on the movie even more than Elvis's filming accident [Laughs]. Daniel, can you blame me?

Hell, na [With a SERIOUS look on his face], with Raquel around, I would be like, "So, Raquel, while they are carting Elvis off to the hospital, why don't you and I go sit under this shady tree that I saw on the other side of that hill? We can share a great sandwich that my momma packed for me...[Laughs]!"

[Laughs] Well, she was a memory that I won't forget, that's for sure. I see Raquel every once in awhile, and we talk about those old days. And, once we had Elvis's injury and stitches taken care of, it was no big thing! But, you know, the press makes a big thing out of everything. The next day, Elvis was out working again.

That's right, he was walking around with that band-aid on, and they even filmed the scenes with him wearing it!

Well, it worked because they shot the fight scene, and so people naturally said, "Okay, Elvis got hurt in the fight scene."

Yeah, it would only make sense. ♦

■ **TRIVIA QUESTION** / View answer on next page

In which one of Elvis's personal books can these personal notes by Elvis be found? "...God loves you, but he loves you best when you sing."

Up Close and Personal:
Shooting at the World's Fair

A candid conversation between Joe Esposito and Daniel Lombardy

Daniel: Tell me about the time you guys were shooting the movie It Happened At The World's Fair...how difficult was it making a movie surrounded by the huge crowds of people which were already attending the "real" Seattle 1962 World's Fair that was going on during the time of shooting?

Joe: When we heard that we were going to be making a movie where they were having the World's Fair up in Seattle, Washington in 1962, all right in the middle of the Fair's daily action, all the guys around Elvis said, "Boy that's gonna be tough," because the producers wanted to film Elvis's movie right in the middle of everything that was already happening! ...I mean, it makes you sweat when you think about the logistics of shooting in a sea of people like that! It was really hard to do that; but luckily we pulled it off without a hitch. If you remember seeing the pictures that were taken off-camera, you can see the mob of people that was all around us. It could have been pretty bad if that situation had gotten out of hand. At least we had those little golf carts to jump into and get through the crowds with. ...They came in handy, and we went everywhere in them.

Did Elvis get a lot of autograph requests from the people who were around the filming while attending the Fair's events?

Yes, he sure did, and Elvis, being the way he was, would always stop and give autographs. That's just what he did. ...He would always make time

---

■ **TRIVIA ANSWER** / Answer to question on previous page
Through the Eyes of the Masters.

to stop for autographs (and give us a damn heart attack in the process!). But, that's just the way he was. So, yeah, shooting there was tough. …So, thank God, the people were pretty good and respected that we were making a movie there. Shooting there was interesting and really a lot of great fun.

Always On My Mind

My name is Mike Piazza, and Elvis has always been an important focus in my lifetime because of the music that I play, and Elvis is always included. I know that there are many stations across the United States that have entirely dropped the "Oldies" format of playing songs from the rock 'n' roll years. Not very often, you may still hear Elvis's, such as "Burning Love" or some of the more recent Elvis songs; but, Elvis's music is always a preference for me. Elvis, in that way, is always with me in my life.

During my radio show every week I always play at least three or more Elvis songs during our three-hour span, if not more. I do a feature called the Countdown where I take a Top Ten hits roster from that date in a year gone by, and Elvis's music is, usually, more than one or two of those songs in that day's particular segment.

I try to play even more Elvis selections by listener request, etc. And, away from work, I am frequently listening to my iPod when I'm driving in my car. There are so many Elvis songs in its list that chances are great that I am always gonna hear Elvis's music when I'm in my vehicle. I put it on "shuffle", and that way, I ensure that an Elvis song will always come up.

■**TRIVIA QUESTION** / View answer on next page
Who was the person that customized the ELVIS BUS?

And, if I am surfing the channels on my home TV when I see that an Elvis movie is on the air, I stop switching the channels and always stop to watch his movie. That's what always happens in my house. I really enjoy it anytime opportunities present themselves for me to listen to or watch Elvis's performances. I am definitely a very big Elvis Presley fan! I've just gotta watch him. I mean, Elvis is always there. I will go as far as to tell you that, on my night table next to my bed, every year I get a new Elvis calendar with his stories, the pictures, the trivia questions and all the memories. So, absolutely, Elvis is right there nearby in my room. In my den, I've a great guitar with a picture of Elvis in its middle. So, Elvis remains in my life each and every day! ◆

Always On My Mind

My name is Glenn Korsinski, and I live in Prague. I have, ever since I can remember, been an Elvis fan. I listen to his music in my car, in my house, and even when I go jogging. My favorite songs are "Crying in the Chapel", "Burning Love" and "What Now My Love". My favorite movies are the "Rockumentaries"…especially *Elvis On Tour*. I have been to Graceland several times, and every time I choke up when I see his grave. I really hope that Elvis takes time out every once in a while when he is "performing" in Heaven! ◆

Did You Know?

That Scotty Moore crashed the pink and black Cadillac into an oncoming pickup truck. ◆

■ **TRIVIA ANSWER** / Answer to question on previous page

George Barris

Ask Joe

Fritz Meyer from Munich, Germany writes:

Joe, I recently returned from Memphis and wondered, "Did the Memphis Mafia ever go out to eat at any of the local restaurants while Elvis was in Memphis? Surely the restaurant owners would have made provisions to setup a private room knowing Elvis was coming, right?"

Yes, that is true; but we didn't go out to eat very often when we were in Memphis. Usually, back in the 1960's, there was this pizza place called Coletta's. We used to go over there and get a pizza and hang out quite a bit. Otherwise, we mostly ate at home because Elvis employed his own personal cooks at Graceland twenty-four hours a day…so there was no reason to go out to eat. But, once in a while, just to get a pizza, where we used to go was Coletta's. ◆

What Really Happened?

Interview Excerpt with Joe Esposito

Reporter: Is it true that Elvis had secondary glaucoma in his left eye, and that it was so bad once that his ophthalmologist, David Meyer, had to stick a needle in his eye to relieve the pressure?

Read Joe Esposito's answer to this question and many others in Volume 3 of the "Celebrate Elvis" series.

■ **TRIVIA QUESTION** / View answer on next page
Why did Elvis get fired from Loews five weeks after returning to work there?

Two NEW releases *from Joe Esposito that compliment each other…and the legendary career of ELVIS PRESLEY!*

Longtime Elvis insider and right hand man, Joe Esposito, lends his invaluable insights and memories to this exciting new series that will set you up and set you straight!

CELEBRATE ELVIS is just that… a celebration of Elvis's career, his life and his legacy. Loaded with fun stories, interviews, trivia and contributions from you, the fans.

CELEBRATE ELVIS is an uplifting, feel-good book that enlightens, entertains and informs!

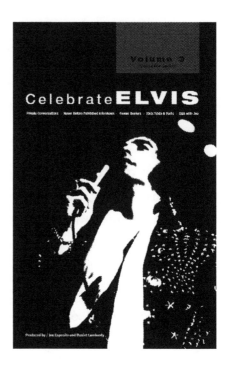

Available at:
www.celebrateelvis.com
and your nearest bookstore

■ **TRIVIA ANSWER** / Answer to question on previous page
It was due to an altercation with another usher.

For the first time ever...**ELVIS-STRAIGHT UP!**

■**TRIVIA QUESTION** / View answer in volume 3

Who introduced Tom Hulett and Jerry Weintraub to Colonel Parker before they formed Concerts West?

Also Available

Remember Elvis
Produced by Joe Esposito

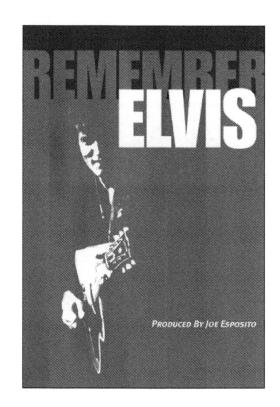

REMEMBER ELVIS is an all-encompassing, in-depth look at the life and career of a man whose popularity is unrivalled in the history of show business and who continues to attract millions of new fans each year.

This ground-breaking book is brimming with rare interviews, insights and experiences, previously unrevealed…until now.

At the heart of this landmark project are over 200 interviews with many of Presley's most intimate associates, as well as some of the biggest names in the film and recording industries.

Available at:
www.tcbjoe.com
and your nearest bookstore

Lightning Source UK Ltd.
Milton Keynes UK
UKHW030612280519

343447UK00007B/778/P